THE TOTAL ROCK KEYBOARDIST

>> A Fun and Comprehensive Overview of Rock Keyboard Playing

JOE BOUCHARD
SHEILA ROMEO

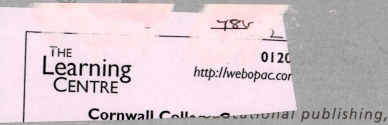

...ational publishing,

and the National Guitar Workshop,

one of America's finest guitar schools, have joined

forces to bring you the best, most progressive

educational tools possible. We hope you will enjoy

this book and encourage you to look for

other fine products from Alfred and the

National Guitar Workshop.

Alfred Publishing Co., Inc.
16320 Roscoe Blvd., Suite 100
P.O. Box 10003
Van Nuys, CA 91410-0003
alfred.com

ISBN-10: 0-7390-4312-9 (Book & CD)
ISBN-13: 978-0-7390-4312-7 (Book & CD)

This book was acquired, edited and produced
by Workshop Arts, Inc., the publishing arm of
the National Guitar Workshop.
Nathaniel Gunod, acquisitions, managing editor
Burgess Speed, editor
Matthew Liston, assistant editor
Timothy Phelps, interior design
Joe Bouchard, music typesetter
CD recorded by Collin Tilton at Bar None Studios, Northford, CT
Thanks to Seth Zowader for his contributions to this book.

Cover photographs:
Electronic keyboard courtesy Korg USA, Inc.
Inset photo ©Ken Settle

Table of Contents

About the Authors

PHOTO • BRETT VERMILYEA

Joe Bouchard is one of the founding members of the legendary rock band, Blue Öyster Cult. He joined the group in 1970 and was a creative member for 16 years. He recorded 13 albums with Blue Öyster Cult for Columbia Records, and was awarded nine gold albums and two platinum albums. Even though he recorded bass parts on every album, he occasionally overdubbed keyboard parts in the studio, especially on many of the songs he wrote.

After leaving Blue Öyster Cult, Joe performed as a touring organist and pianist with Spencer Davis of the Spencer Davis Group. He has performed on stage with many top artists including J. Geils, Mike Watt, Marty Friedman of Megadeth and former Doors members, Robbie Krieger and Ray Manzarek. Joe recently released his first self-produced CD, *Solid Citizens*, with his band, The X Brothers, on Cellsum Records.

Joe is the author of *Rock Guitar for Beginners* (Alfred/National Guitar Workshop #14854) and *No Reading Required: Easy Rock Bass Lines* (#23226). He also hosted *Rock Bass for Beginners* (#21933), an instructional video. He holds a bachelor of music education degree from Ithaca College, and a master of music degree from the Hartt School at the University of Hartford.

A classically trained pianist with the heart of a rocker, **Sheila Romeo** has a keen interest in everything from music by the great composers of centuries past, to rock, new age and classical music performed by the many talented artists of today. Sheila graduated *cum laude* from Berklee College of Music in 1992 where she studied keyboard and majored in music production/engineering and music synthesis.

Sheila's classical background and love of rock music naturally translate to the genre of progressive rock. She has studied and played in the styles of Steve Walsh (Kansas), Rick Wakeman (Yes), Tony Banks (Genesis) and Keith Emerson (Emerson, Lake and Palmer). She has played on many studio sessions and projects, as well as in several bands.

As an audio engineer, Sheila worked at various recording studios in the Boston area. She has worked with major label artists, including Peter Wolf, Aimee Mann and various rap and R&B artists on Island Records.

Introduction

Welcome to *The Total Rock Keyboardist*. Whether you're a beginning, intermediate or advanced player, this book teaches everything you need to know to rock out on the keys. While this book reviews all the basics, it will be helpful if you have already begun playing and reading music, at least to the level of *Alfred Basic Piano Method, Lesson Book 2*.

If you are an intermediate or advanced keyboardist, you may be tempted to skip the beginning chapters. However, you can still benefit from practicing this material. If an exercise is too easy for you, try transposing it into different keys. This will help you become more familiar with the keyboard. Or, use the exercise as a starting point for your own musical improvisations.

The use of a keyboard in rock started in the early 1950s rock 'n' roll era. The hard-driving piano that propelled early rock 'n' roll was influenced by the blues, jazz, R&B, gospel and country styles. After World War II, people needed to get up and dance, often in a loud and boisterous manner. Radio, and the proliferation of electronic instruments, made rock music accessible to everyone.

Some said it was the work of the devil, but the first rock 'n' roll pianists came from the revivalist gospel churches. Jerry Lee Lewis set out to prove that the piano could be just as much a forerunner in sonic evolution as the electric guitar. Little Richard, with his flamboyant personality and hard rockin' style, played the piano with an intensity never seen before. With all the joy and youthfulness of this musical style, once it got started, it just couldn't stop.

Electric organs, originally designed for churches, were brought into rock music because they could be louder and were usually easier to transport than a traditional piano. Ray Manzarek of the Doors was a major champion of the rock organ. Not only did he play great keyboard parts, but he also covered the bass part with his left hand, leaving great spaces for their guitarist and singer to get creative with.

The electric piano became popular late in the 1950s. This was another great texture for keyboard players to use in rock bands. The invention of the clavinet (a funky, synthesized harpsichord sound) came in the 1960s as rock styles evolved further into funk and soul music. In the 1970s, the evolution of the synthesizer took keyboards to the next level. Progressive rock bands featured keyboard parts of unprecedented complexity and originality. Now, a rock keyboardist can create whatever their knowledge and imagination will allow.

Be sure to listen to as many different kinds of music as you can, both on recordings and at live performances. Your rock chops will expand exponentially with each new musical experience you have. Keep your mind and ears open to ideas used by classical and jazz composers, and to the sounds of music from other cultures. Rock music is only limited by your imagination, and your imagination is only limited by your experiences.

This book is designed to be fun while giving you a sense of rock 'n' roll history. You will also get a feel for the rhyme and reason behind why music "works." If you master all the material in this book, you will be able to play out in any rock keyboard situation. Just practice as much as you can, listen constantly to all kinds of music and play with enthusiasm and confidence.

Roll up your sleeves and let's get started.

A compact disc is available with this book. Using the disc will help make learning more enjoyable and the information more meaningful. Listening to the CD will help you correctly interpret the rhythms and feel of each example. The symbol to the left appears next to each example that is performed on the CD. Example numbers are above the symbol. The track number below each symbol corresponds directly to the song or example you want to hear. Track 1 provides an "A" note in case you need to tune your keyboard.

Chapter 1: Getting Started

Sitting at the Keyboard

Good posture and hand position are extremely important. Start on a comfortable but firm chair or bench. The height of the chair should put your elbows on the same level with the keyboard. As you depress the keys, your fingers should be slightly curved—as if holding a ball.

Standing at the Keyboard

Rock keyboard playing gives the performer more leeway with posture than classical keyboard playing. Because rock music requires a high energy level, many keyboardists prefer to stand. Besides, a standing performer is more visible to the audience and you don't want the guitar players to hog all the glory! The biggest drawback to this approach is that it becomes more difficult to play the pedals, so you'll notice that many rock players use pedals sparingly. If you are going to stand, raise the level of the keyboard so that your elbows are on the same level with the instrument, just as in the seated position.

The Keyboard

Every musical sound, or tone, is represented by a *note*. On the keyboard, each note has a key that is given a letter name, A through G. After G, the sequence repeats. The keyboard, especially one that is full-sized like a piano, includes a wide range of pitches and notes, from very low to very high. You can play the bass, the chords, the melodies and all parts in between. Let's look at the basic keyboard:

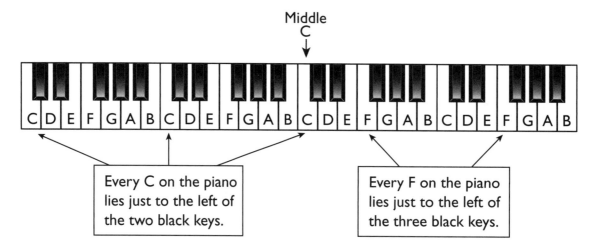

Every C on the piano lies just to the left of the two black keys.

Every F on the piano lies just to the left of the three black keys.

Music Notation—Pitch

Pitch has to do with which note we play and its degree of highness or lowness. Learning to read music involves making a mental connection between the note on the keyboard and the notes on the page. We write music on five lines and four spaces. It is easy if we see the horizontal lines as a big grid that tells us how high (toward the right side of the keyboard) or how low (toward the left side) the notes are from the center. That grid of five lines and four spaces is called the *staff*. In keyboard music, two *staves* are often connected in a *grand staff*—one staff for each hand.

Compare the notes on this grand staff to the keyboard diagram on the previous page.

The Grand Staff

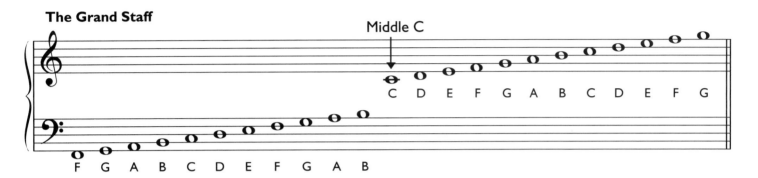

At the beginning of each staff, there is a symbol called a *clef*. The *treble clef* 𝄞 is for the high-pitched notes, usually played with the right hand (**R.H.**). Its curly end surrounds the "G" line. For this reason, it is sometimes called the *G clef*.

The *bass clef* 𝄢 is for the lower-pitched notes played with the left hand (**L.H.**). The two dots surround the "F" line. For this reason, it is sometimes called the *F clef*.

Clefs designate the relative highness or lowness of the tones and help keep the notes organized on the lines. As you become more familiar with these symbols, recognizing the names of the notes will become much easier.

Ledger Lines

We use *ledger lines* to write notes that are higher or lower than those that fit on the staff. They are short lines that extend the staff either higher or lower.

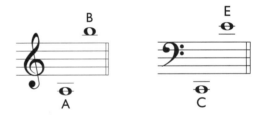

We can use just about any number of ledger lines to write very high or very low notes, but the more ledger lines there are, the harder it is to read the notes at a glance. Ledger lines become easy to read with experience. If you must, count the lines up or down by letter names until you find the name of the note, then mark it with a pencil. This will help you memorize the ledger line names.

Middle C

Middle C is a major "landmark" on the keyboard. If you know where it is, you'll never be completely lost. It sits on a ledger line between the treble and bass staves.

Accidentals

The white keys on the keyboard are the *natural*, or unaltered, notes. The black keys on the keyboard are called *accidentals*. They can either have a *sharp* (♯) name or a *flat* (♭) name. The letter name is determined by the adjacent note. When the natural note (white key) is raised one key to the right (higher in pitch), we use the sharp name. When the natural note is moved one key to the left (lower in pitch), we use the flat name. For example, the black note to the right of D is D♯. The black note to the left of E is E♭. Notice they both use the same black key. Notes that sound the same but have different names are called *enharmonic equivalents*.

This black key can be either E♭ or D♯.

This black key can be either G♭ or F♯.

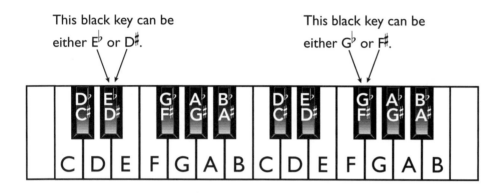

When a note is made sharp or flat, it stays that way until something happens to make it natural again. Notes are returned to their natural position with a natural sign (♮).

This is what accidentals look like on the staff.

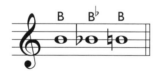

Two more accidentals that are less frequently used are the *double flat* (♭♭) and *double sharp* (𝄪). They raise or lower the pitch of a note by two keys on the piano. For example, C𝄪 is the same pitch (enharmonic) as D. In most cases, this note would be notated as D, unless the song is in an unusual key such as D♯.

Music Notation—Time

Note and Rest Values

Pitches are played in a framework of time to organize the music and make it come to life. A system of *note values* and *rest* (silence) *values* has been developed over the centuries to show how long to play a note or how long to be silent.

The basic unit of time in music is a *beat*. Each note is held for a specific amount of time that is measured in beats. For example, a *quarter note* ♩ usually lasts for one beat. Beats are the basic pulse behind music. To the right is a chart of the basic note values.

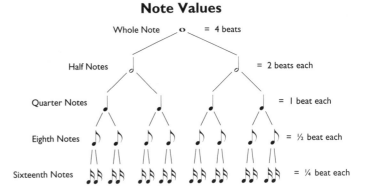

Rest values have the same structure as note values (see the chart to the right).

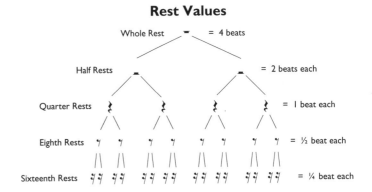

Measures and Barlines

The staff is divided by vertical lines called *barlines*. The space between two barlines is called a *measure*. Measures (sometimes called *bars*) divide music into groups of beats. A *double bar* marks the end of a section or example. The *final bar* signals the end of the piece of music.

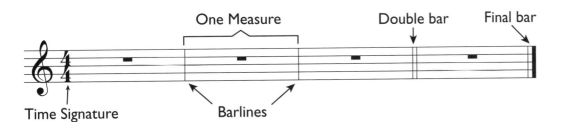

Time Signature

Each piece of music begins with a *time signature*. The numbers in a time signature tell us how to count time in the musical piece or song. The bottom number shows the kind of note that equals one beat (4 indicates a quarter note; 8 indicates an eighth note, etc.). The top number shows how many beats are in each measure.

4 = Four beats per measure
4 = The quarter note ♩ = one beat

6 = Six beats per measure
8 = The eighth note ♪ = one beat

Beams

Some of the notes on the previous page were designated with *flags* on their *stems*.

Beamed eighth notes

Count: 1 & 2 & 3 & 4 &

We can connect the stems with fat lines called *beams* to make them easier to read when seen in a group. To the right are examples of *beamed notes*. Notice the counting numbers underneath the notes. Eighth notes divide the beat into two equal parts and are counted "1-&, 2-&, 3-&, 4-&." Sixteenth notes divide the beat into four equal parts and are counted "1-e-&-ah, 2-e-&-ah, etc."

Beamed sixteenth notes

1 e & ah 2 e & ah

Ties

A note or rest value can be increased by using a *tie*. A tie is a curved line that connects two or more notes of the same pitch. You would play the first note and hold it for the duration of the first and second notes together. In other words, do not strike the tied note—just continue to hold the first note for the tied note's value. On the right are some tied notes. Notice the counting numbers below the staff. Don't sound the notes that fall over the counting numbers in parentheses.

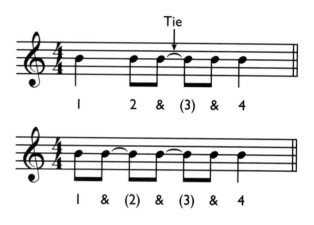

Tie

1   2 & (3) & 4

1 & (2) & (3) & 4

Notes can be tied over barlines, as in the example to the right.

1   2   3 & 4 & (1) (2)(Rest on 3 & 4)

Dots

The *dot* increases the value of the note by one half of its given value. For example, a half note (two beats) with a dot would increase by half the value of a half note (one beat), so a dotted half note equals three beats (2 + 1 = 3). Here are some dotted notes:

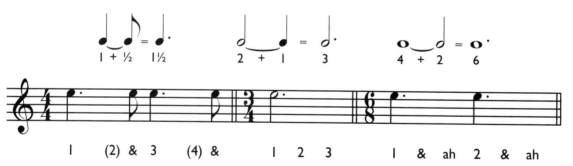

1 + ½   1½   2 + 1   3   4 + 2   6

1   (2) & 3   (4) &   1   2   3   1 & ah 2 & ah

Notice that in $\frac{6}{8}$, the six eighth notes can be divided into two beats, each containing three eighth notes. Instead of counting 1–2–3–4–5–6, count 1 & ah, 2 & ah. So, we can say that in $\frac{6}{8}$, the dotted quarter note (equal to three eighth notes) equals one beat. There are then two beats per measure.

Triplets

A *triplet* is a group of three notes played in the time of two notes with the same value. For example, two regular eighth notes divide a beat into equal parts. An *eighth-note triplet* divides a beat into three equal parts. A *quarter note triplet* divides two beats into three equal parts.

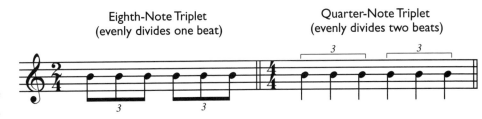

Eighth-Note Triplet (evenly divides one beat)

Quarter-Note Triplet (evenly divides two beats)

Other Important Symbols and Info

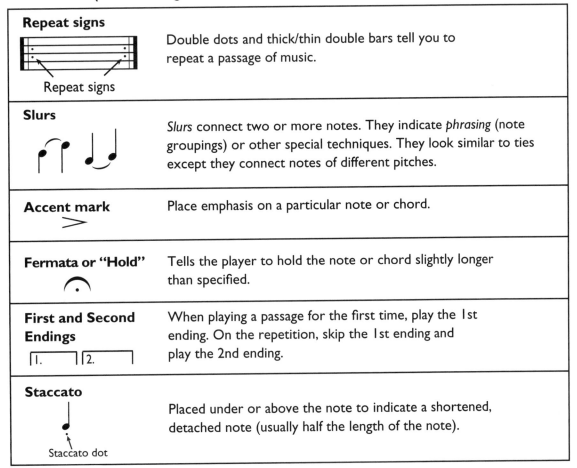

Repeat signs	Double dots and thick/thin double bars tell you to repeat a passage of music.
Slurs	*Slurs* connect two or more notes. They indicate *phrasing* (note groupings) or other special techniques. They look similar to ties except they connect notes of different pitches.
Accent mark	Place emphasis on a particular note or chord.
Fermata or "Hold"	Tells the player to hold the note or chord slightly longer than specified.
First and Second Endings	When playing a passage for the first time, play the 1st ending. On the repetition, skip the 1st ending and play the 2nd ending.
Staccato	Placed under or above the note to indicate a shortened, detached note (usually half the length of the note).

Fingering

Playing the keyboard smoothly often requires that you use specific fingers in a specific order. Fingerings for the right hand are placed above the notes. Fingerings for the left hand are placed below the notes. Here are the numbers of the fingers, the thumb being "1" for both hands, the index finger "2" for both hands, etc.

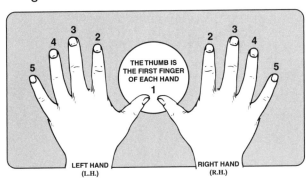

THE THUMB IS THE FIRST FINGER OF EACH HAND

LEFT HAND (L.H.)

RIGHT HAND (R.H.)

Practice Tip

You should practice with a metronome or drum machine to keep the *tempo* (the relative speed of the music) steady. Keeping a solid beat is very important, especially in a rock band.

At the beginning of each example you will find a metronome marking like this: ♩ = 72.

This means the quarter note, or one beat, will proceed at a tempo of 72 beats per minute. While you can play the examples faster or slower than the marked tempo, the tempo marking will give you a point of departure. It is a good idea to start practicing much slower and work up to the recommended tempo.

Half Steps and Whole Steps

Understanding the keyboard is made easy with a system of measuring the distance between two or more notes. These distances are called *intervals* and the most basic of these are *half steps* and *whole steps*. The diagrams below show how these intervals relate to the keyboard.

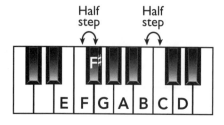
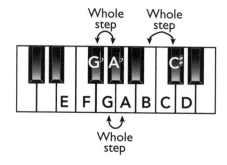

The Major Scale

A *scale* is a group of notes organized in alphabetical order. Scales are the building blocks of harmony and melody. Every type of scale is organized with a specific arrangement of whole steps and half steps. The most important scale by far is the *major scale*. Below is a major scale starting on C, the C Major scale, and the formula of whole steps and half steps.

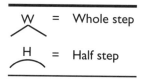

C Major Scale

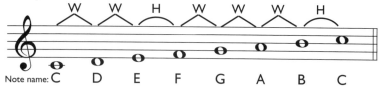

This formula of intervals will create a major scale no matter which note you start from (the first note of a scale is the *tonic*, or *root*). However, starting on any note other than C will necessitate the use of accidentals. You will find it necessary to use either sharps or flats, but never both. The note names must always progress in alphabetical order. Below is a D Major scale. Notice that to create the whole step between the 2nd and 3rd degrees, you must use an F♯. The same situation arises between the 6th and 7th degrees. Check it out:

D Major Scale

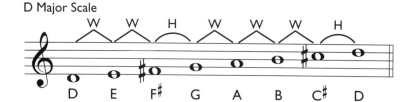

Intervals

All the notes of a major scale are given *scale degree* numbers based on their distance from the root. They are all given *quality* names: either *major* or *perfect*. In this system, a whole step up from the root of the scale is called a *major 2nd*. In fact, any whole step is called a major 2nd. Here are the major and perfect intervals in relation to the root of a C Major scale. The numbers below show the distance measured in half steps.

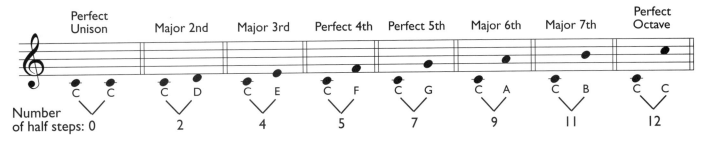

Any major interval can be lowered by a half step to become a *minor* interval. The 4th can be raised a half step to become an *augmented 4th*, and the 5th can be lowered a half step to become a *diminished 5th*.

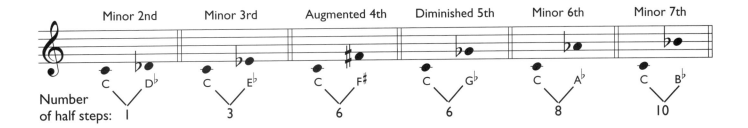

As you construct chords and other scales later in the book, these concepts become very important.

Refer to the chart below to learn the numbers and interval names based on size in half steps.

Chart of Intervals

Degree	Number of Half Steps	Interval	Abbreviation
1	0	perfect unison	PU
♭2	1	minor 2nd	min2
2	2	major 2nd	Maj2
♭3	3	minor 3rd	min3
3	4	major 3rd	Maj3
4	5	perfect 4th	P4
#4 *	6 ("tritone")	augmented 4th	Aug4
♭5 *	6	diminished 5th	dim5
5	7	perfect 5th	P5
#5	8	augmented 5th	Aug5
♭6	8	minor 6th	min6
6	9	major 6th	Maj6
♭7	10	minor 7th	min7
7	11	major 7th	Maj7
1	12	perfect octave	P8

* The augmented 4th and diminished 5th intervals are enharmonically equivalent and are sometimes called a *tritone* because they are equal to three whole steps.

Exercise: Try forming each of these intervals going both up and down from different notes on the keyboard. Play them both *melodically* (one note at a time) and *harmonically* (both notes at the same time).

Chapter 2: Rock Music Theory

Keys, Key Signatures and Why We Use Them

Each rock tune revolves around a specific pitch we call the *tonal center*. That pitch is the *root* of the *key*. The root, or *key note*, will be the root of the scale that is used to create the song. If a C Major scale was used, then we are *in the key of C*. Even in a simple song, the music may stray away from the key, but it usually comes back to a satisfying ending or, to use baseball terminology, "home plate."

To indicate keys in written music, key signatures are used. A key signature is a group of sharps or flats shown at the beginning of a line of music. It is comprised of either sharps or flats, never a combination. The accidentals in the key signature are automatically applied throughout the song. For example, a flat on the B line represents B♭.

This tells us that every B in the tune is played B♭ unless otherwise indicated with a natural sign. This is a great type of shorthand; it saves writing out all those accidentals. It also tells us in a heartbeat that the key is F, because only the F Major scale has just a B♭.

The sharps or flats in a key signature are derived from the major scale. For example, the key signature for D Major will include F♯ and C♯ because those are the accidentals that occur when we build a major scale starting on D. See the cycle of 5ths chart below for all the key signatures.

D Major Key Signature

Cycle of 5ths

The *cycle of 5ths* (also known as the circle of 5ths) helps us understand how keys relate to each other. Often, songs can shift keys in midstream. Knowing how the keys relate, and which accidentals to look out for, is important. Notice that if you go clockwise around the circle, or up by 5ths, a sharp is added to each key: G has one sharp, D has two, A has three, etc. If you go counterclockwise around the circle, up by 4ths (or down by 5ths—it's the same thing), a flat is added to each key: F has one flat, B♭ has two, etc.

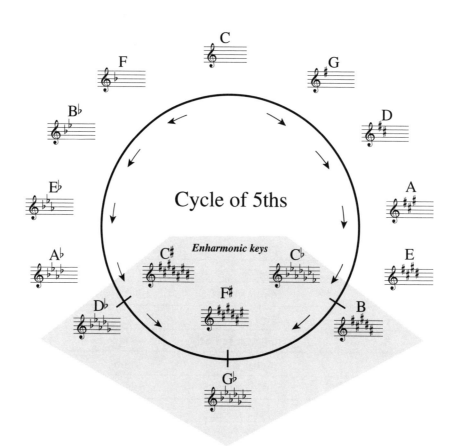

Major Scale Fingerings

A *fingering* is a specific order of fingers to use in a tune or scale. Learning any major scale fingering will help you get comfortable with its key. Playing scales is also a great exercise for building up your keyboard technique.

Here is the right-hand fingering for the C Major scale:

* Notice that the 4th note is played by crossing your thumb underneath fingers 2 and 3. This allows you to finish the scale using the fingers in order: 1, 2, 3, 4 and 5. Since there are eight notes in the scale, and you only have five fingers, you'll always have to cross the fingers.

Here is the left-hand fingering for the C Major scale:

** In the left-hand fingerings, the 3rd finger crosses over the 1st finger to play the 6th note.

Practice the right and left hands hand separately. When you've mastered both, play them together.

C Major Scale

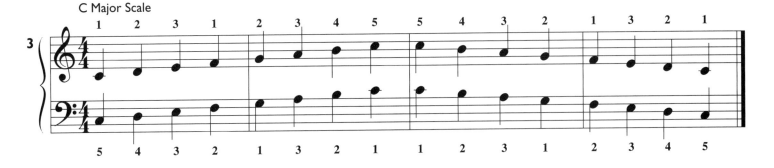

The 12 Major Scales

All 12 of the major scales are shown below. You should learn how to play each of these scales ascending and descending, with both hands.

While it is important to learn all of the keys, the most common rock keys are C, G, D, A, E, F and B♭.

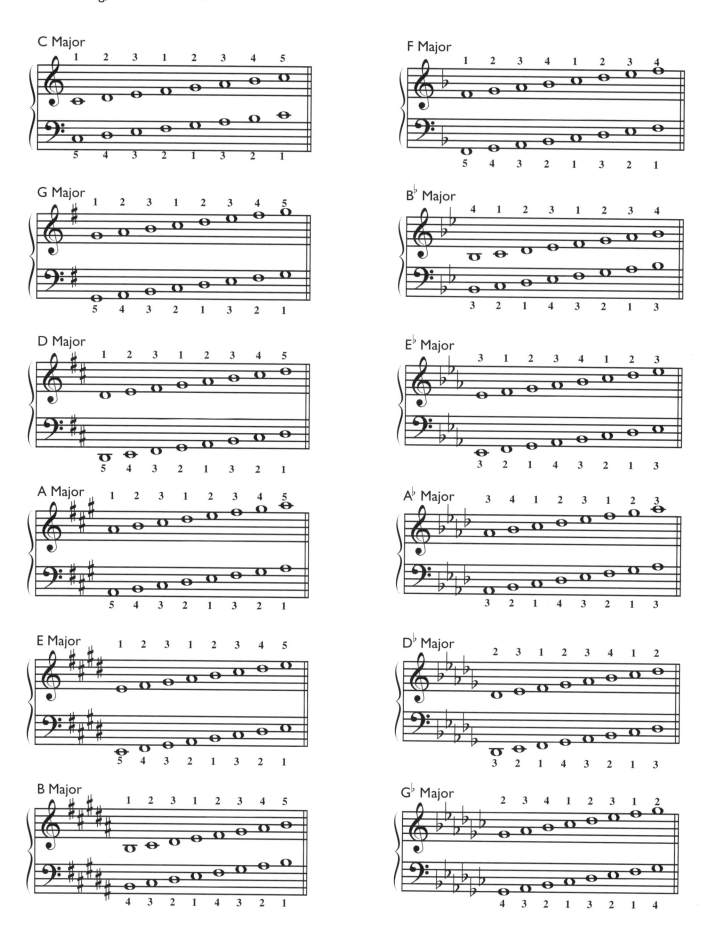

Minor Scales and the Relative Minor

Minor keys have a distinctively darker, sadder and possibly more intense sound than major keys. All minor scales are closely related to a major scale. The 6th degree of any major scale is the root of a minor scale. For example, if you count up to the 6th degree of a C Major scale, you'll arrive at A. Now, if you play the notes of the C Major scale, but start and end on A, you will have played the A *Natural Minor* scale. This kind of minor scale is called "natural minor" because the notes of its *relative major* scale (the scale it was derived from) are left unchanged.

R = Root

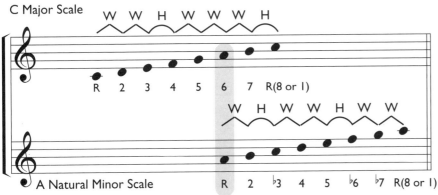

The natural minor scale has a different pattern of whole steps and half steps than the major scale. Compared with the major scale, the 3rd, 6th and 7th scale degrees of the minor scale are one half step lower. We refer to these scale degrees as ♭3, ♭6 and ♭7.

The key of A Minor is the *relative minor key* to C Major. Every major key has its corresponding minor key.

MAJOR KEY	RELATIVE MINOR
G	E
D	B
A	F♯
E	C♯
B	G♯
F	D
B♭	G
E♭	C
A♭	F
D♭	B♭
G♭	E♭

The 12 Minor Scales

All 12 of the minor scales are shown below. As with the major scales, you should learn how to play each of these scales ascending and descending, with both hands.

The most common minor keys for rock music are A Minor, E Minor, D Minor and G Minor.

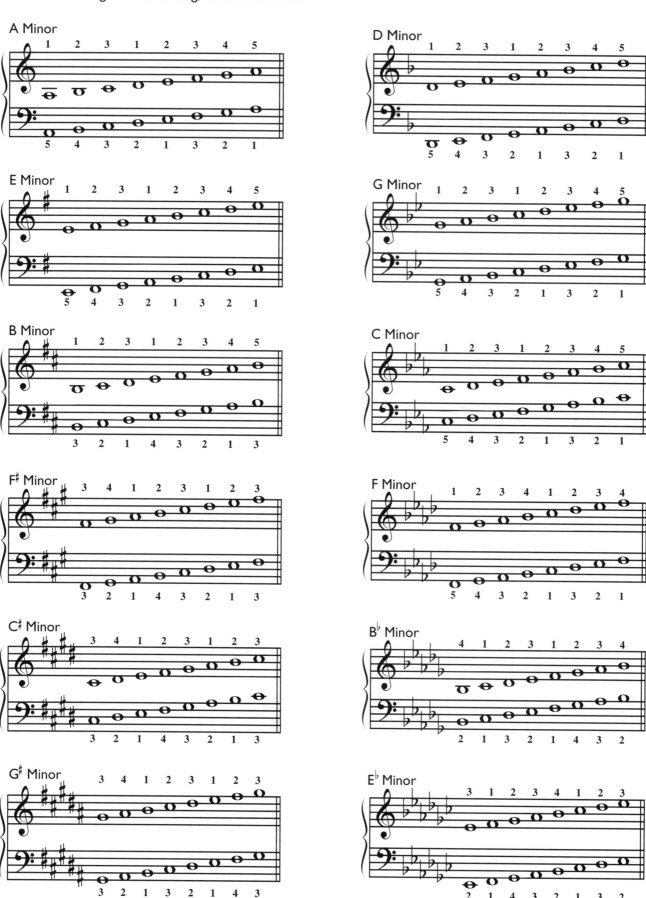

Chapter 3: Chords

The Workhorse of Rock: the Triad

A *chord* is a group of three or more notes played together. A *triad* is a three-note chord. Most rock music uses triads. Triads are derived from the major scale and are built with intervals of a 3rd. For example, if you play the root, 3rd and 5th of a C Major scale, you will create the C Major triad. It's that easy!

Let's check the intervals used in the C Major triad (in rock lingo, we would simply say "C chord").

All major triads have the same formula of interval relationships:

1 = The root.

3 = The middle note or 3rd of the chord (a major 3rd above the root).

5 = The upper note or 5th of the chord (a minor 3rd above the 3rd or a perfect 5th above the root).

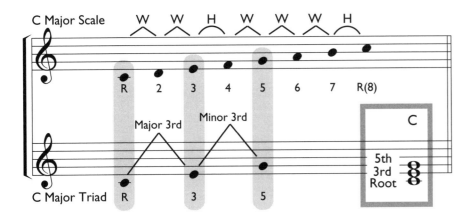

We built our C chord on the root of a C Major scale. We can build similar triads on the root of any major scale. Let's build a few more chords. Notice how all major chords have the same formula: major 3rd on the bottom, minor 3rd on top.

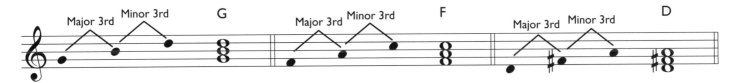

Here is a good exercise for learning the major chords. The chord names are written above the music. Notice that chords with sharps in their names can also be called by their flat names. For example, C♯ can also be called D♭,

A♯ can also be called B♭, and so on. Once you've learned these chords with your right hand, try playing them an octave lower with your left hand.

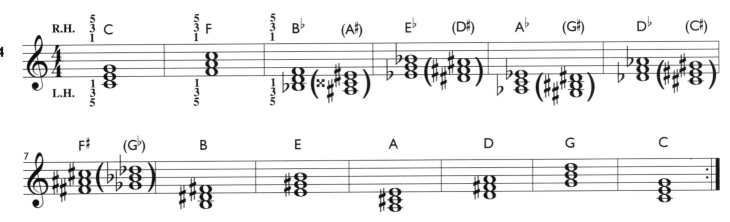

Below is a tune that uses major chords. The right hand plays mostly eighth-note triads and the left hand plays single notes. Follow the counting under the treble clef staff.

Practice Tip: Don't forget the repeat sign in bar 8. Go back to the beginning and play the first eight measures again. Then, continue to the end. Also, there is a fermata (see page 11) on the last chord.

Track 2 *Babylon*

mf = Mezzoforte. Moderately loud.

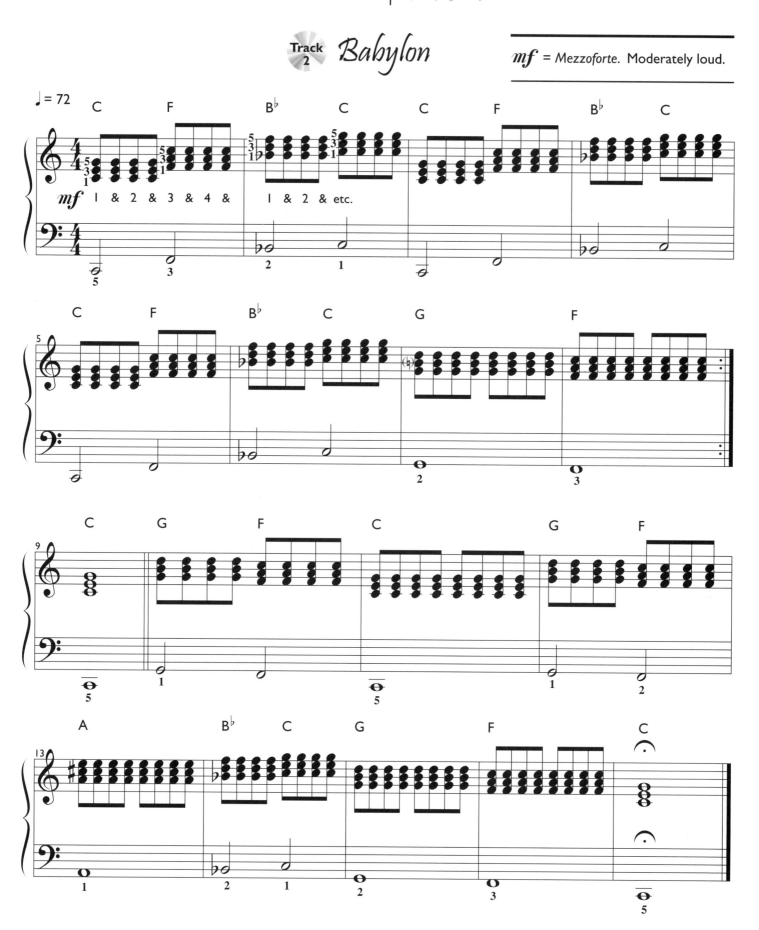

Minor Chords

Like major chords, minor chords are derived from scales. The formula for a minor triad is: 1–♭3–5 (see right).

1	=	The Root.
♭3	=	The middle note or flat 3rd of the chord (a minor 3rd above the root).
5	=	The upper note or 5th of the chord (a major 3rd above the flat 3rd or a perfect 5th above the root).

The example below shows how a minor triad can be derived from the 1st, 3rd and 5th degrees of a minor scale.

A Natural Minor Scale

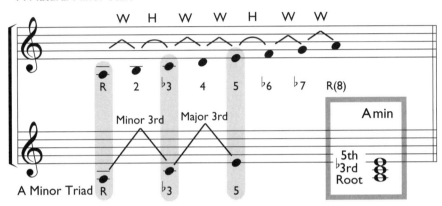

Below is an example comparing a C Major chord with a C Minor. Notice how the major triad can be made minor by lowering the 3rd. In sheet music, this chord is known as Cmin or Cm.

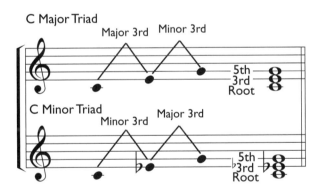

Below is an exercise to help you get acquainted with minor chords. Notice the chords are ordered in a cycle of 4ths (descending cycle of 5ths). After you practice this with the right hand, play it an octave lower with the left hand.

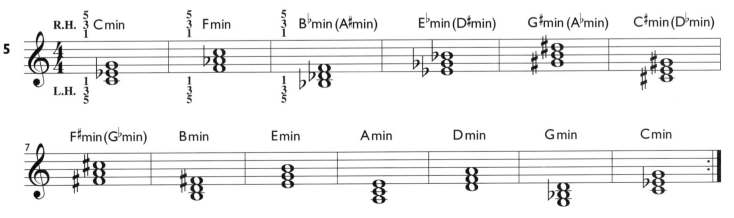

"House of the Rising Sun" is a traditional tune in the key of A Minor. Notice that it includes the A Minor chord. Eric Burden and the Animals recorded this song in the 1960s, and it became an instant rock classic. Their arrangement featured a great rock keyboard part. In the arrangement provided here, the first section has the vocal melody in the right hand. The second section has chords in the right hand and a single-note bass line in the left.

This tune uses the $\frac{12}{8}$ time signature. There are 12 beats in each measure but we think of them in groups of three, with 1, 4, 7 and 10 being the "strong" beats (slightly accented). The result is really four beats per measure with each beat divided into three eighth notes (count 1-&-ah, 2-&-ah, etc.). This is called a *compound meter*. Four beats per measure with each beat divided into two eighth notes, $\frac{4}{4}$, is called a *simple meter*.

Here is how the rhythm to this song is counted:

The first note in this tune is a *pickup note*, which is a note that occurs before the first full measure. This one comes on the "ah" after beat "4." This incomplete measure is always balanced by an incomplete measure at the end.

f = Forte. Loud

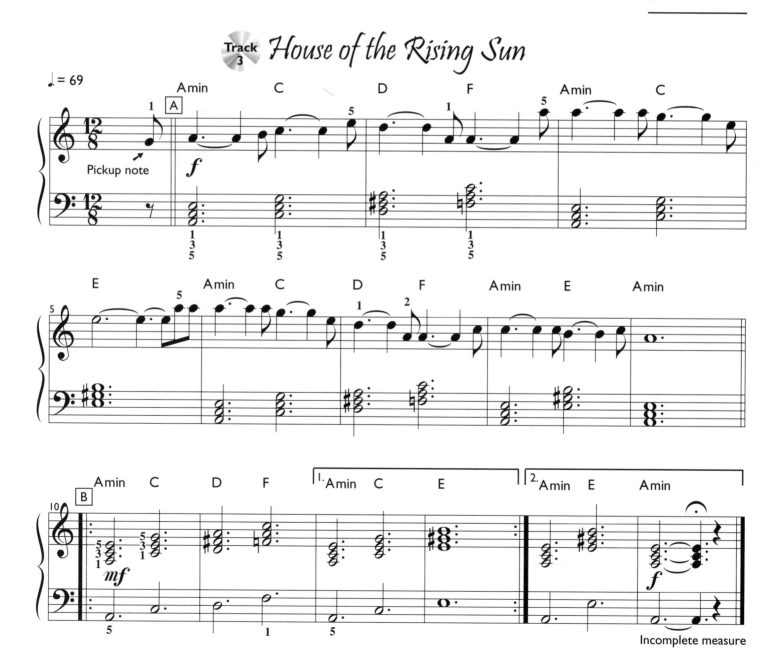

Incomplete measure

Major and Dominant 7th Chords

Most early rock tunes use simple major and minor triads, but occasionally rock players will spice things up by using *7th chords*. A 7th chord is a four-note chord. If you take a triad and add a tone a 7th up from the root, you have a 7th chord. You can also think of it as adding another 3rd above the 5th of a triad.

Let's look at a C Major triad with a 7th added above the 5th.

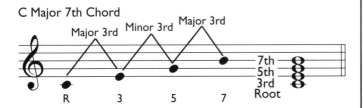

In sheet music, this chord is known as CMaj7 or CM7.

If you build a 7th chord starting on the root of any major scale and using only notes from that scale (C Major in the example above), the result is a *major 7th chord*. The major 7th chord is a sweet-sounding chord. Once in a while, we sneak it into rock tunes. Red Hot Chili Peppers use a major 7th in "Under the Bridge" with great effectiveness.

In rock, the bluesy sounding *dominant 7th chord* is more commonly used. This kind of 7th chord has a ♭7 or minor 7th—the 7th is lowered one half step. The example below shows the formula for this cool sounding chord. Play it loud. Dominant 7th chords rock.

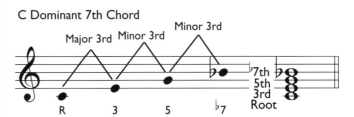

In sheet music, this chord is known as C7.

The exercise below will give you some practice with dominant 7th chords. After you play it with the right hand, play it an octave lower with the left.

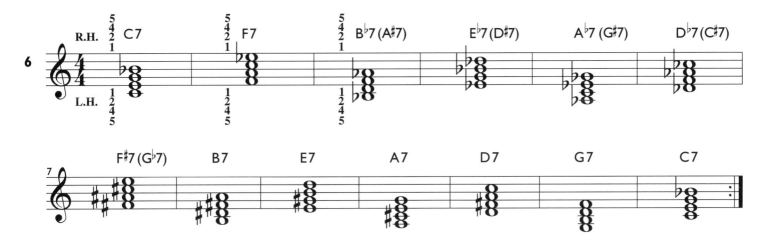

Let's play a tune using dominant 7th chords.

First Call

(*Last time only)

Minor 7th Chords

Just as we add a ♭7 to a major chord to create a dominant 7th chord, we can add a ♭7 to a minor chord to create the four-note minor 7th chord. The example below shows the formula for a minor 7th chord.

C Minor 7th Chord

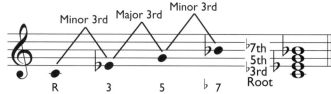

In sheet music, this chord is known as Cmin7 or Cm7.

The following exercise will give you some practice with
minor 7th chords. After you play it with the right hand,
play it an octave lower with the left.

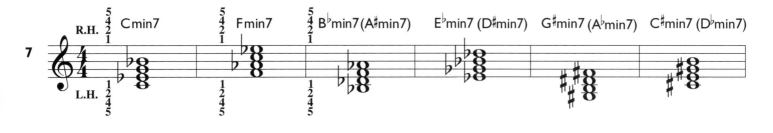

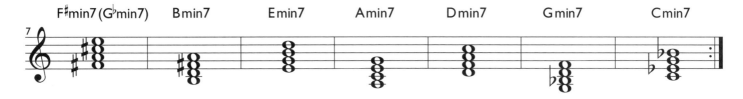

Here's a fun tune to play using min7 chords:

Isle of Dreams

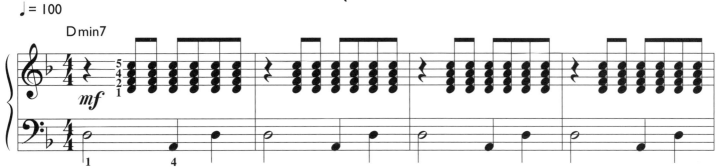

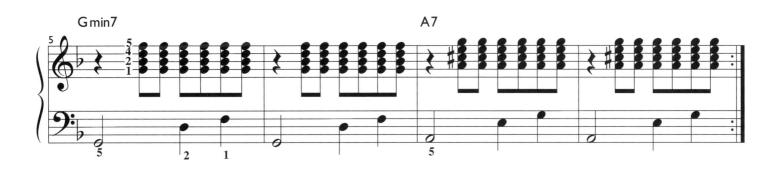

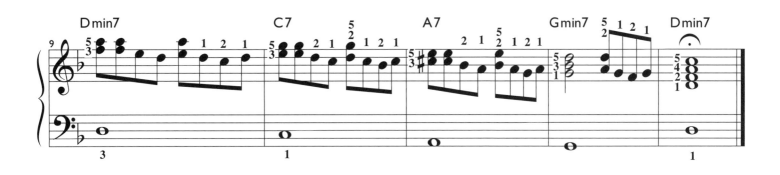

Chapter 4: An Introduction to Rock Rhythms

The success of a good rock tune has a lot to do with strong rhythms. It doesn't take long to understand this concept if you hear a great live rock band pumping the music along at full tilt. A great band will always have a great sense of rhythm.

This style of music grew up in a time where unschooled or minimally trained musicians liberally borrowed the best rhythmic ideas from jazz, early blues and boogie-woogie. Boogie's repetitive bass lines were tossed into a stew with a dash of country simplicity making a rhythmic dish that became known as rock 'n' roll. By pointing this musical feel at the emotions of the teens of the 1950s and 1960s it became, and still is, one of the most popular musical styles ever.

Here are two ways to develop your sense of rhythm:

1. Make sure the time, or pulse, of the music is as steady as a ticking clock. Play along with your favorite recordings, or use a metronome or similar device.

2. Make sure everyone in your band feels the rhythm together. Listen carefully as you play.

Syncopation

Often, the difficulty in reading rhythms lies in the fact that music on the printed page *looks* harder than it actually is. This is because of *syncopation*, the shifting of the accent to a weak beat or weak part of a beat. In $\frac{4}{4}$ time, beats 1 and 3 are strong beats; beats 2 and 4 are weak. The *offbeats*—the "&s"—are the weak parts of the beats. The *onbeats*—where we count the numbers (1, 2, 3, 4)—are the strong parts of the beats.

To understand the concepts of offbeats and onbeats, you should study your feet. If you stomp your feet to the beat of a song with a steady rhythm, you learn that there are onbeats (when your foot is firmly planted on the floor) and offbeats (when your foot is lifted off the floor).

Below is a diagram of feet doing what they do to good rock music.

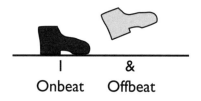

1	&
Onbeat	Offbeat

In the example below, play a note on each onbeat, keeping the beat very steady.

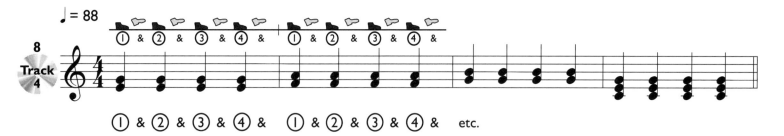

Good! But, after a while, rhythm like this can sound stiff. You may need more of that rock 'n' roll, rhythmic punch.

Try the following. It includes some syncopation. The second accent is moved half a beat to the right of the second beat. The accents fall on beat 1 and the "&" of 2.

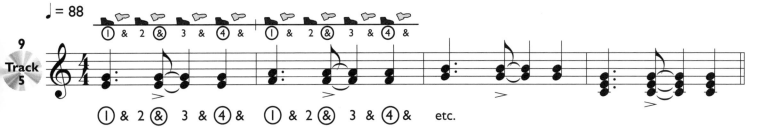

Use your metronome or drum machine. This will help you keep a steady tempo and make it easy to find the onbeats.

This seems simple enough. But, syncopation often looks difficult on the printed page because it is frequently accomplished with ties. We read two notes when only one is sounded. If you write the beats under the music, it will be easier. As in the examples printed on this page, write the numbers with their "&" symbols (1 & 2 & 3 & 4 &). This will help you determine if you should play on an onbeat (1, 2, 3, 4) or an offbeat ("&"). You'll be rockin' in no time at all!

Here is another syncopated example using ties:

Let's combine a straight quarter-note rhythm in the left hand with syncopations in the right hand. Be careful to keep the left hand steady as you play the accents in the right hand. One of the most important things to learn when playing keyboards is independence between the hands.

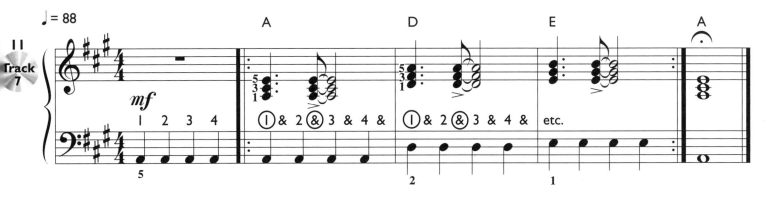

Rhythmic Independence

An essential skill that a keyboardist must master is the ability to play two different rhythms simultaneously—one in the left hand and one in the right. Practice each tune very slowly, one hand at a time. Then, put the hands together, also very slowly, until each hand feels independent of the other. Finally, try a faster pace.

Over the Top

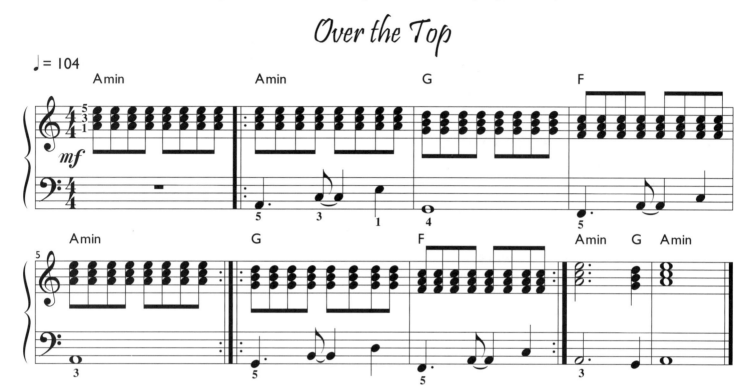

This exercise has syncopations in the right hand and steady eighth notes in the left.

Under the Depths

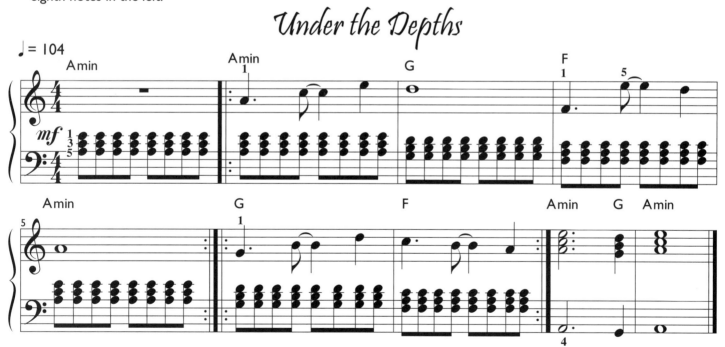

After a bit of practice, the concept of syncopation becomes much easier. The trick is not to panic when you see the dots and ties, but to work things out with some simple counting. Always include the "&" in your counting. This is called *subdividing*. Use a pencil and mark the onbeats and offbeats in the music.

This chapter has been an introduction to syncopations using eighth notes. On page 54, we will look at syncopations using sixteenth notes, the kind that funk players build their songs around.

Chapter 5: Basic Bass Lines

It's the night of the big gig. You're on the bandstand, ready to rock out with your killer keyboard parts. Suddenly the band leader turns to you and says: "Bad news… the bass player's car broke down. He's stuck in the breakdown lane of the Jersey Turnpike. He's not gonna make it tonight. Your left hand is the bass player now. Good luck!" At this point, you either break into a cold sweat and run out of the room screaming, or you open your massive mental file of cool bass lines and say, "Let's rock!"

Rock music always has strong bass lines. In the early days of rock 'n' roll, pianists like Jerry Lee Lewis and Fats Domino played hard rockin' left-hand bass lines—often borrowed from barrelhouse or boogie-woogie piano—that vigorously drove the music forward.

A rock keyboardist might be called upon to double the bass guitar part for an even more solid bottom-end sound. The Doors, the legendary 1960s act led by Jim Morrison, never had a bass player in concert. Ray Manzarek's left hand on a Fender keyboard provided their bass. As the scenario above suggests, you may have to play bass on a synthesizer or keyboard sampler someday, so let's learn some left-hand patterns.

The simplest left-hand part might be just holding the left hand in whole or half notes while the right hand plays the chords (see "Babylon" on page 20). It's more likely, however, that you'll need to lay down some rockin' rhythms. Here are a few classic patterns. Count carefully to master the syncopated rhythms.

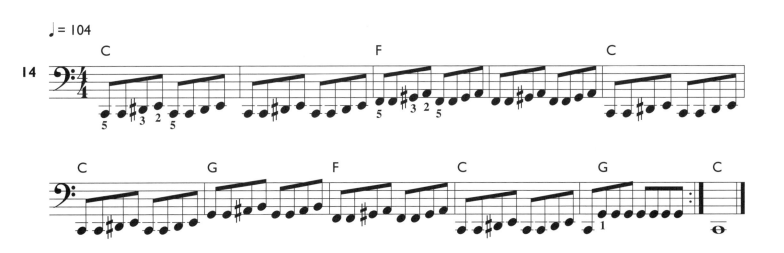

Let's put some of those patterns together in a song. The boxed letters (A, B, C, etc.) above measures 1, 9 and 14 designate important sections of the song. This is what musicians are talking about when they refer to the "A section" or the "B section" of a tune.

Get 'Em Up

Chapter 6: Arpeggios and Chord Inversions

Arpeggios are "broken" chords. On the keyboard, this is a simple matter of playing chords in varying patterns, up and down, mostly one note at a time.

Following are some common arpeggio patterns. Play these with the right hand and then an octave lower with the left hand.

Notice the next example is written in bass clef for the left hand. Play it an octave higher with the right hand as well.

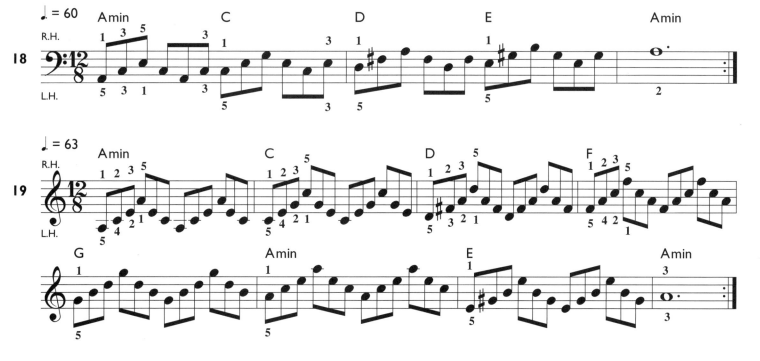

You first learned "House of the Rising Sun" on page 22. Here's your old friend back again, this time as an *accompaniment*, or backing part, with arpeggios.

House of the Rising Sun
Arpeggios

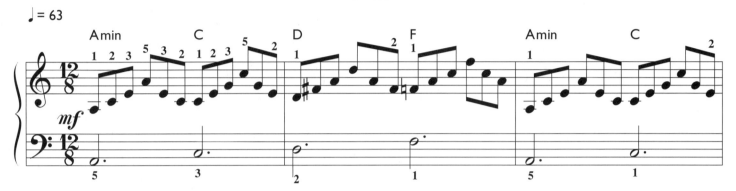

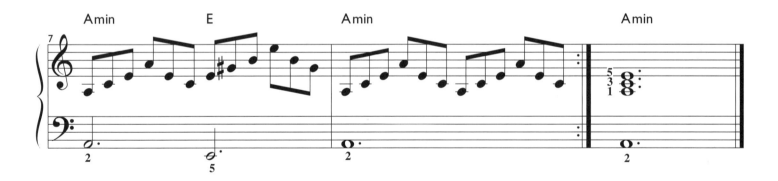

Chord Inversions

So far, in this book, we've played all our chords in *root position*. In other words, the root is the lowest note of the chord. But chords are often *inverted*. When a chord is inverted, something other than the root is the lowest note.

If the 3rd of the chord is on the bottom, it is said to be in *1st inversion*.

If the 5th of that chord is on the bottom, it is said to be in *2nd inversion*.

We have good reasons for using inversions:

1. To make the chord easier to finger and make smoother changes from one chord to another

2. To make the chord sound higher or lower without going into the next octave

3. To make smooth bass lines

Here are four different major chords and their inversions:

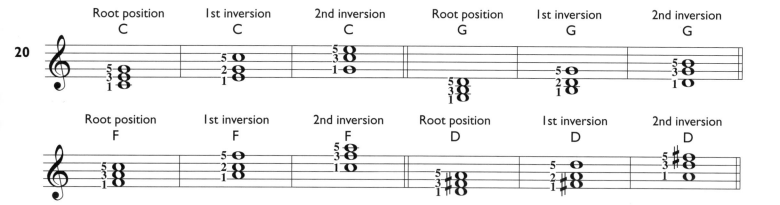

Minor chords are inverted in exactly the same way. Here are two different minor chords and their inversions.

The lowest note of the chord always determines the inversion. We can play an inversion with the right hand, but it is not truly an inversion if the left hand is playing the root. Below are a few inversions for both hands. Notice that a triad can be spread out so that the three notes are split up between the hands. Furthermore,

it is important to note that the left hand is often doubling a note that is also being played in the right hand. Virtually any combination of the chord tones is possible, although some may be more desirable than others. In the end, your ear will be your guide. This important aspect of music is called *voicing*.

Slash Chords

In rock music, you will often see chord symbols with a slash (C/G, Dmin/C, F/D, etc.). A *slash chord* tells you there is an inversion lurking about. For instance, C/E tells you there is a 1st inversion C chord. C is the chord name and the lowest note is an E. The E is the 3rd of the chord.

Slash chords can aid in building totally different and interesting harmonies. For instance, C/D is a C chord with a D in the bass. The D is not a chord tone, so it makes for an interesting, colorful chord.

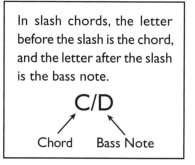

In slash chords, the letter before the slash is the chord, and the letter after the slash is the bass note.

C/D

Chord   Bass Note

You will find that many inversions feel easier to play than the same chord in root position. Here is a tune you learned on page 20 but arranged here to include inverted chords. Compared with the original, this new version moves more smoothly from chord to chord. This is an example of good *voice leading*. Each note of each chord moves a shorter interval to each note of the next chord. It sounds better and is easier to play.

Back to Babylon

♩ = 92

mp = Mezzo piano. Moderately soft

7th Chord Inversions

Just as major and minor triads can be inverted, four-note 7th chords can be inverted. The difference is that since they have four notes, they can be inverted three times. The *3rd inversion* has the 7th as the lowest note of the chord. Inversions are usually notated as slash chords.

"Down to Earth" uses inversions of both dominant and minor 7th chords. Note the stepwise motion of the bass line.

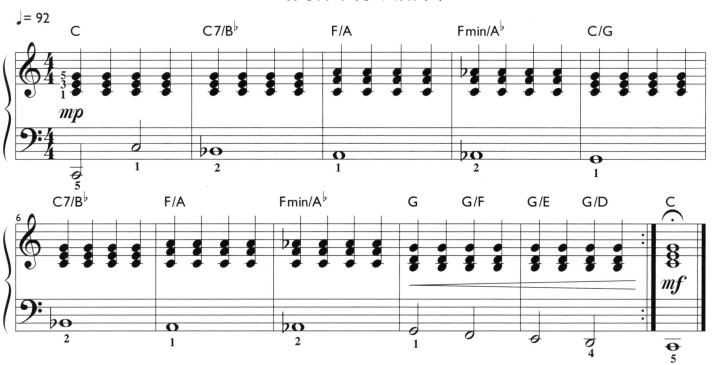

Down to Earth

Pedal Tones

It is a common rock technique to change chords in the right hand while holding a single, unchanging note in the left hand. As the chords change, *dissonance* (a clashing sound) occurs causing tension and, often, suspense. The unchanging note in the left hand is called a *pedal tone*. The term "pedal tone" is taken from an organ technique where the performer holds down a floor-pedal note with a foot while playing a series of chords with the hands above the held note. Pedal tones are discussed in more detail on page 95.

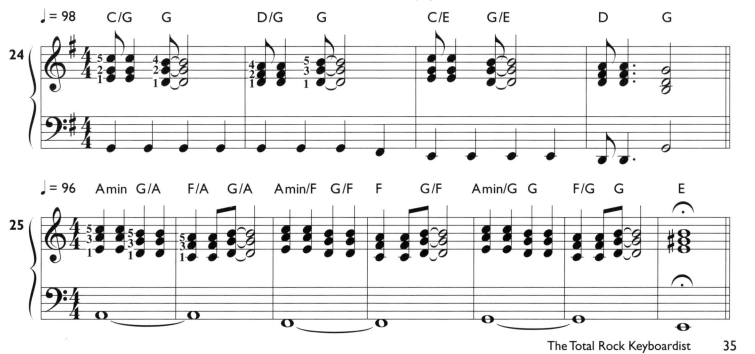

Chapter 7: More Left-Hand Patterns

Boogie-Woogie Patterns

Boogie piano developed as an outgrowth of the raucous barrelhouse piano of the early twentieth century. This style relies on a strong, percussive bass line to drive the songs forward and makes you want to move your feet. Here is a classic left-hand line in quarter notes with the added 7th tone.

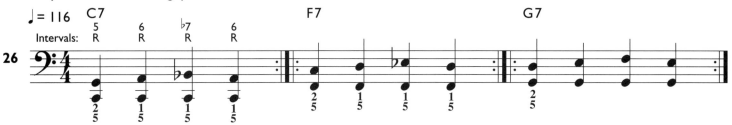

Here is another classic left-hand part. Guitar players are particularly fond of this idea, especially in the keys of A or E. On the keyboard, it's easiest in C.

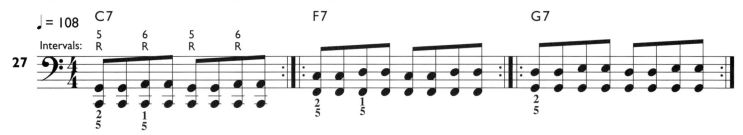

Example 28 is a boogie pattern in G. Strive to keep the pattern very steady with a solid feel. This pattern uses an A♯, which is the same as (enharmonically equivalent to) B♭. The B♭ is the ♭3, or minor 3rd, in G. This pattern highlights the sound of the minor 3rd moving to the major 3rd (B). This minor/major ambiguity is a big part of the language of blues- and boogie-influenced rock 'n' roll.

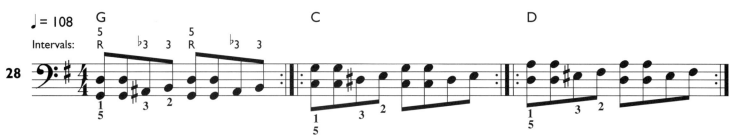

Here is a walking boogie bass line. Let's add a few chord hits to this next pattern. As you add the right hand, keep the left hand very steady.

Walkin' & Talkin'

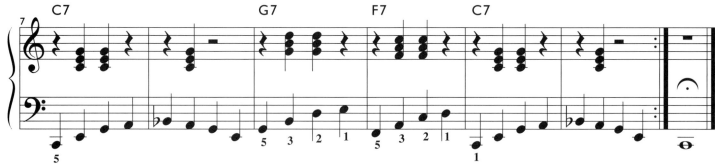

The pattern used in "This Rock 'n' Roll Thing" will rock the house when played with spirit. Repeat the introduction until *you hit a groove* (where the rhythm starts to feel great!), and then add the right-hand part. Pay attention to the first and second endings (see page 11).

Octaves

In keyboard music, octaves are often used to strengthen bass lines in the left hand. They are also used to add emphasis to a melody line in the right hand. Octaves require extra effort and a little stretching of the fingers, especially for players with small hands. If your hands get tired, stop and rest. Some players have to "roll" their octaves—that is, play the lower note and then immediately jump to the higher note. Try playing these scales in octaves using one hand at a time.

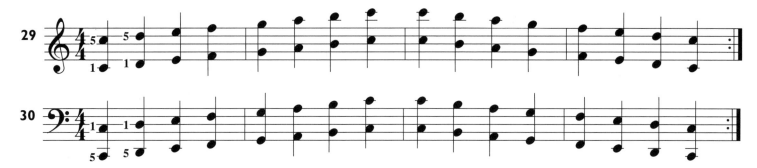

At first, it seems logical that all octaves would be played with a 5-1 fingering in the left hand and a 1-5 fingering in the right hand. However, if your hands can stretch far enough, it is sometimes good to use a 4-1 fingering in the left hand and a 1-4 fingering in the right hand when playing on the black keys. This makes it easier to connect notes with lots of octaves in succession. If this feels too difficult, move on and come back to it later. Following is an A Major scale with 1-4 fingerings on the black keys:

Try a D Major scale in the left hand.

"Almost There" features the use of a *sus4 chord* in the 5th measure. In a sus4 chord, the middle note, or 3rd, is raised a half step to the 4th tone above the root. In this case, the F♯ (3rd) of the D chord is raised to the G (4th). In bar 6, the 4th resolves down to the 3rd. (See page 67 to learn more about suspended chords such as the sus4.)

─── = Crescendo.
Play gradually louder.

Almost There

Broken Octaves

Octaves can be used to make good, simple bass lines by alternating the pinky and thumb to create a rocking-back-and-forth motion in the left hand. Paul McCartney of the Beatles used this technique in songs such as "Lady Madonna" and "Martha, My Dear." Play the tune below featuring this cool technique.

All Night Station

Boogie Lines in Octaves

Here is a classic boogie-woogie line with octaves.

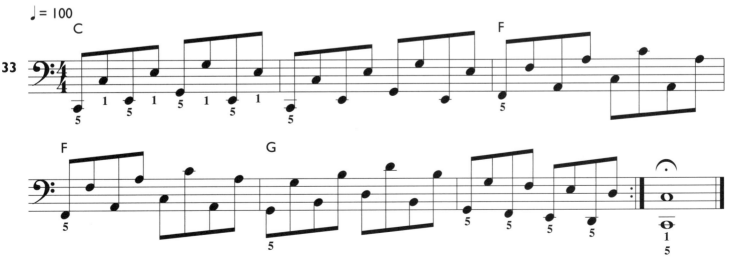

If it feels comfortable, you can try playing every other octave with a 4-1 fingering. If you have an acoustic piano or full-size electronic keyboard, play the left hand one octave lower than written. Also, notice the key signature: four sharps! E Major is a big rock key. So, take it slow at first, but get used to it!

Saloon Spider

Chapter 8: Pentatonic Scales and Beginning Improvisation

So far, we've concentrated on *rhythm section* techniques, such as chords, bass lines and rhythms, which can be used to accompany a singer or lead instrument. Now you're ready to step into the spotlight and learn to *improvise* a solo. Improvising is the act of spontaneous invention, creating music from your own imagination.

Major Pentatonic Scale

One basic method of improvisation is to find a scale that sounds good over the chords being played. *Pentatonic scales* are simple, and they fit like a glove over most basic chords. All pentatonic scales have five notes (*penta* means "five" in Greek).

Over a major chord, the *major pentatonic* scale is a good choice. The chart to the right compares the C Major and C Major Pentatonic scales. They are the same except the major pentatonic scale omits the 4th and 7th.

Try playing a C Major chord with your left hand while playing a C Major scale with your right hand. You will notice that the 4th and 7th (F and B) have a tense or dissonant sound that clashes with the chord. Now, play the C Major Pentatonic scale over the same C Major chord.

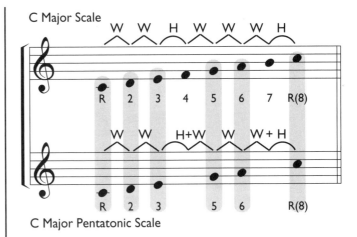

C Major Scale

C Major Pentatonic Scale

Because the 4th and 7th have been omitted, there are no clashes and every note sounds good.

The first time through the tune "Deeper River," play the melody as written. After the repeat, try to improvise a melody of your own using the C Major Pentatonic scale. Experiment with different rhythms and notes of the pentatonic scale. Practice will improve your improvisation skills. If you get "stuck," just play the left-hand part for a couple of measures, and jump in with the right hand when you feel ready.

♩ = 112

Track 8 *Deeper River*

In Example 34, the right hand plays three C Major Pentatonic *phrases*. A phrase is a complete musical thought. Music is like a little conversation, and the phrases are the sentences. Play the three written phrases and then improvise a fourth. Create a melody similar to the other three using the C Major Pentatonic scale. You get the last word in the conversation. Don't worry: you can play any note in the scale. There are no "wrong notes" as long as you stay within the scale. Experiment with different rhythms, and don't be afraid to leave a little space (rests) in your melody. If you have trouble being spontaneous, try writing a melody on the staff.

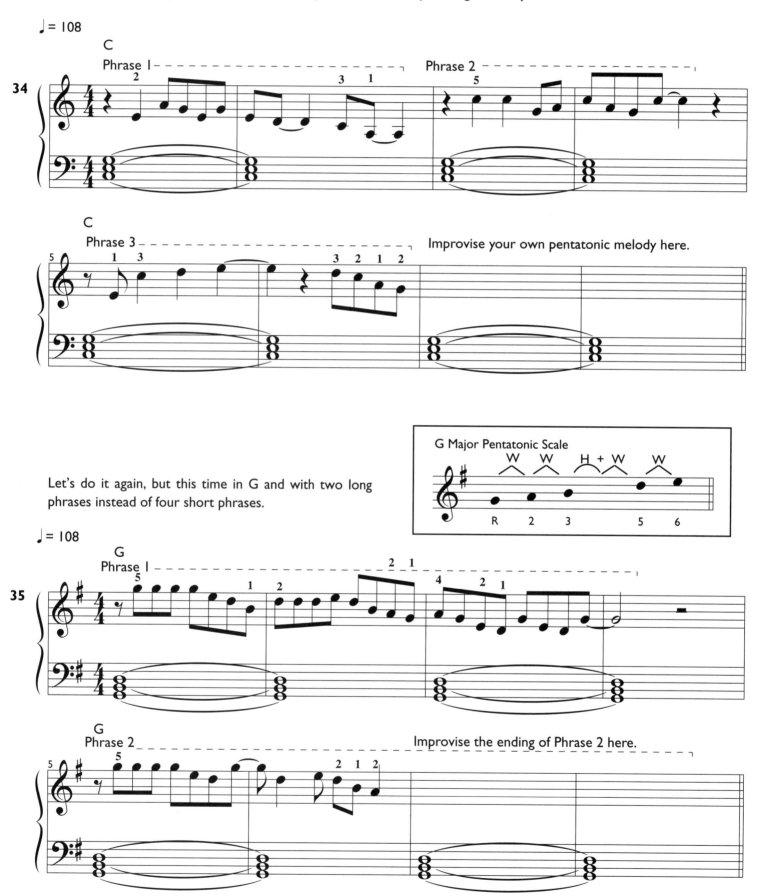

Let's do it again, but this time in G and with two long phrases instead of four short phrases.

In this example, we use a different pentatonic scale for each chord. When the left hand plays a G chord, we play notes from the G Major Pentatonic scale. Over the C chord, we play the C Major Pentatonic. The chords to a song are often called *the changes*. Changing scales as the chords change is called *playing the changes*.

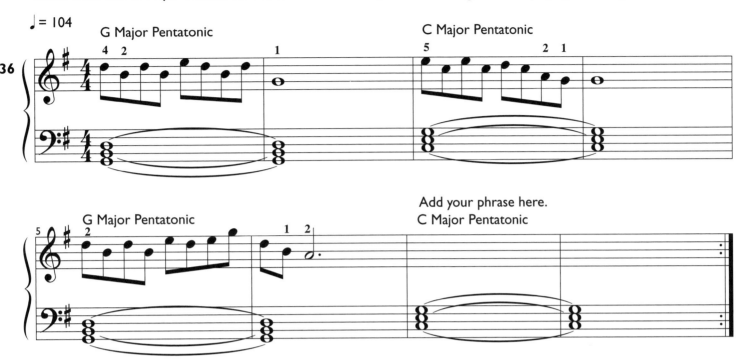

Let's play the changes some more, but in the key of F with two new pentatonic scales: F and B♭. You're on your own—no tune has been provided. Improvise with gusto.

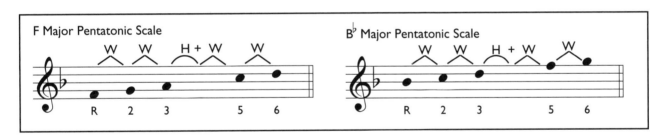

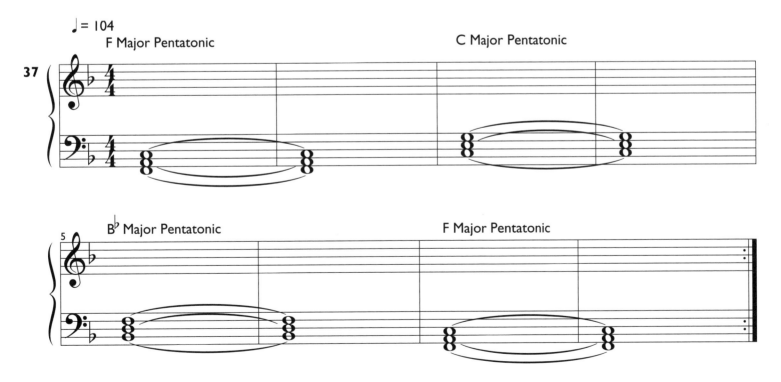

In "Far as You Like," try to determine where the pentatonic scales are changing with the chords. In the repeat of the A section, improvise your own melody in the right hand using these scales:

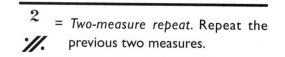

$\overset{2}{\text{※}}$ = *Two-measure repeat.* Repeat the previous two measures.

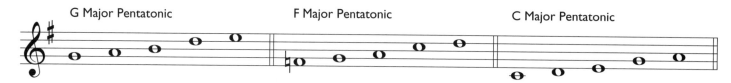

This song features a *coda*, a section played only at the end of a piece. Play through the song until you reach the *D.S. al Coda* marking in measure 14. Then, go back to the *segno* and play, without repeats, until you reach the *To Coda* marking in measure 14. This second time through, go to the coda and play to the end.

Coda
$\oplus$ = Coda

※ = Segno

Minor Pentatonic Scale

The minor pentatonic and major pentatonic scales are closely related but sound very different. The major pentatonic scale has a country music flavor but the minor pentatonic scale has a darker, bluesier sound. They are similar in that they both have five notes, but they compare differently to the major scale.

Below is a C Major scale and a C Minor Pentatonic scale. Notice that the 3rd and 7th of the minor pentatonic scale are flatted (♭3 and ♭7).

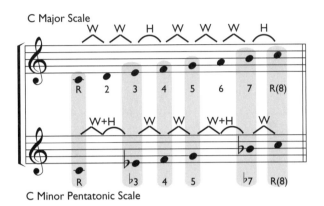

Following is a comparison of the C Major Pentatonic and the A Minor Pentatonic scales. The minor pentatonic scale is related to the major pentatonic scale in the same way that the natural minor scale is related to the major scale (see page 17).

The root of the A Minor Pentatonic scale is built on the 6 of the major pentatonic scale. It is a minor 3rd below the root of the C Major Pentatonic. A Minor Pentatonic and C Major Pentatonic have the exact same notes. Played in a different order, though, they sound completely different.

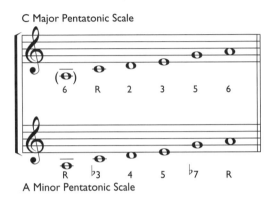

To get a feeling for the minor pentatonic scale, learn to play "New Life." Notice the key signature. This tune is in the key of C Minor.

New Life

"Off the Main Highway" uses the E Minor Pentatonic scale for the main melody. Notice that, except for the first two measures and the last, the song is repeated three times. Improvise your own melody over the repeats using the E Minor Pentatonic scale. Remember, you do not have to stay in the same octave as you improvise. Feel free to move the E Minor Pentatonic scale to different octaves. Have fun.

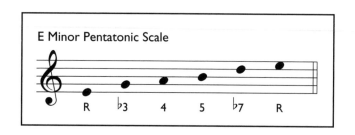

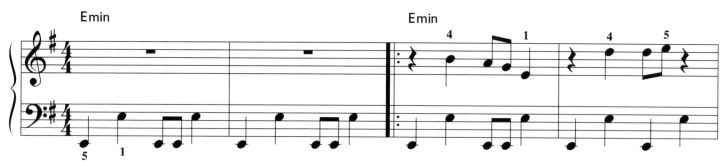

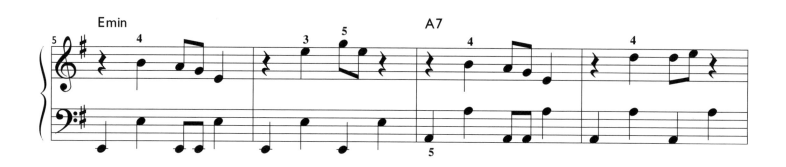

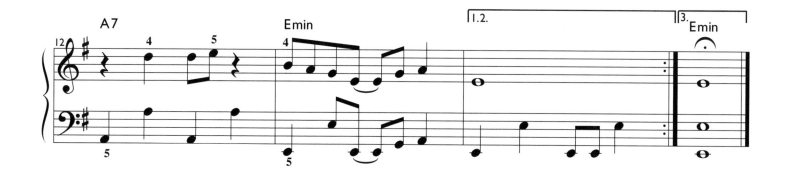

Chapter 9: The Blues

Blues music is at the heart of lots of great rock 'n' roll, so let's take a look at this important musical style.

The Blues Scale and Blue Notes

The major and minor pentatonic scales you learned in the last chapter are great tools for blues improvisation, and so is the *blues scale*. Below, the C Blues scale is compared with the C Major scale. The C Blues scale is very similar to the C Minor Pentatonic scale except it includes an additional flat 5 ($^\flat$5). The $^\flat$5 is a very distinctive sound. It adds such an important twist to the blues sound that it is often called a *blue note*. Sometimes, for reasons of convenience, the $^\flat$5 is written as a $^\sharp$4, its enharmonic equivalent.

C Major Scale

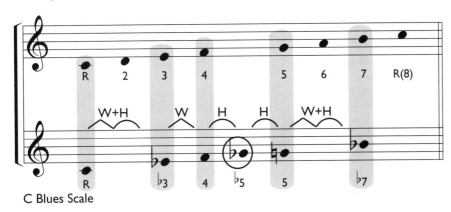

C Blues Scale

Here is a typical blues melody using the $^\flat$5:

Since blues harmony is more open to experimentation than many other musical styles, the blues performer has much more leeway in choosing notes for a solo. Quite often, the blues will freely combine major and minor sounds (major 3rds and minor 3rds) in a piece of music. The left hand might play harmony based on major chords while the right hand, or the soloist, plays a melody based on the minor chord. The minor 3rd ($^\flat$3) played against a major chord is another very important blue note.

Here is a short blues passage in G that typifies this combination of major (in the left hand) and minor (in the right hand).

"See the Light" demonstrates the use of the ♭5 in the key of E Minor.

Track 13 See the Light

Fine

** *Da Capo al Fine* means to return to the beginning and play up until the *Fine*.

*Hold last time only

The Grace Note

The *grace note* is like the spice in Louisiana cooking—a tiny bit goes a long way. Grace notes are little notes that precede a larger note called the *main note*. The two notes are usually connected with a small slur marking. To play a grace note, rob a bit of time from the main note and quickly play it before the main note. Some blues players actually slide their finger off the grace note on to the main note, especially if the grace note falls on a black key. Fingerings such as this are marked with a dash; 3-3 indicates to slide the 3rd finger from one key to the next (see example 40).

To prepare for grace notes, play the exercise below. Notice that the ♭5 blue note is sometimes written as A♯ (if it is ascending) and sometimes as B♭ (if it is descending).

This time, three of the blue notes are shortened to become grace notes. In each case, quickly slide your finger off the black key to the white key. Don't worry about being rhythmically precise with the grace notes. There is some rhythmic freedom allowed in this style. The main thing is to have fun and "get the blues."

Diatonic Triads

To understand how the blues really works, we must learn about *diatonic triads*. Diatonic means "of the scale," so diatonic triads are those triads that come from the scale. Each scale degree has its own chord which is assigned a Roman numeral. Notice in the example below that each note of the scale becomes the root of a chord.

Diatonic Triads in C

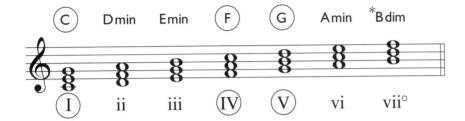

The first (I), fourth (IV) and fifth (V) chords of the major scale are the most important chords in blues and rock music. There are thousands of songs that contain only these three *primary chords*. As long as we've got the primary chords, rock 'n' roll will never die!

Upper case Roman numerals are used to indicate major chords. Lower case Roman numerals are used to indicate minor or diminished* chords.

---

* B Diminished Triad

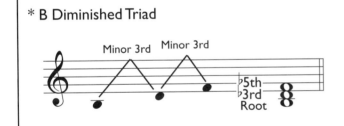

Notice the vii° sign under the last chord in the example above. The little circle means "diminished." A diminished triad, written *dim*, is made up of two minor 3rds stacked above the root. The diminished triad occurs naturally on the 7th degree of the major scale. Play the diminished triad shown. It has a very distinctive flavor.

The concept of diatonic chords can be carried into all key signatures. Here are the diatonic triads for the D Major scale.

Diatonic Triads in D

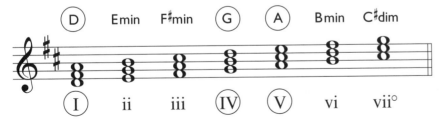

Practice the diatonic chords in all key signatures, building a triad on each note of the scale. You'll find all the major scales on page 16 of this book, and a helpful chart of the primary chords in every key on page 50.

The 12-Bar Blues

Most blues songs, and most blues-based rock songs, have a structure we call the *12-bar blues*. Obviously, the form is 12 bars long. The form can be repeated as many times as you like. Each time through the 12-bar form is called a *chorus*.

Using Roman numerals to identify the chords, here is the formula for a basic 12-bar blues (see right):

4	measures of	I
2	measures of	IV
2	measures of	I
1	measure of	V
1	measure of	IV
2	measures of	I
12	measures of	blues!

This chord pattern is the universal language of the blues, and all rock players should know it in all key signatures. Here is a 12-bar blues in G:

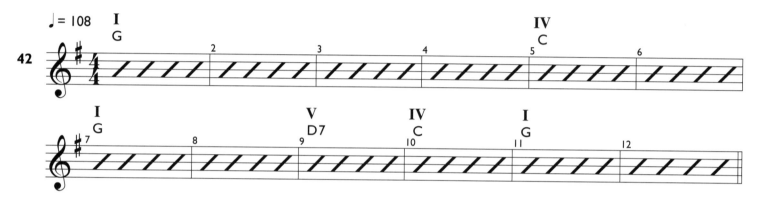

For practice, play this blues with simple triads.

Transposing

Using the Roman numerals, it is possible to move this chord progression to any key. This is called *transposing*. You can start on any triad and apply this formula, and you'll be playing the blues. Every day, try playing this pattern in another key. Follow the cycle of 5ths order. A seasoned player will know the blues in any key.

The chart to the right will help you play the blues in any key.

Primary Chords in All 12 Keys

Major Key	I	IV	V
C	C	F	G
G	G	C	D
D	D	G	A
A	A	D	E
E	E	A	B
B	B	E	F#
G♭	G♭	C♭	D♭
D♭	D♭	G♭	A♭
A♭	A♭	D♭	E♭
E♭	E♭	A♭	B♭
B♭	B♭	E♭	F
F	F	B♭	C

Variations on the 12-Bar Blues

Often, players will spruce up the standard 12-bar blues (example 42) with variations. The form is still 12 measures long, but other chords will be substituted for the basic chords.

 = *Slash notation*. Play the chords for the indicated number of measures, using any rhythm that sounds good.

The Quick Four

This first pattern moves to the IV chord in the second measure. This common blues variation is sometimes called a *quick four*. The rest of the chords remain the same.

Notice that to get a true blues sound, we use dominant 7th chords throughout.

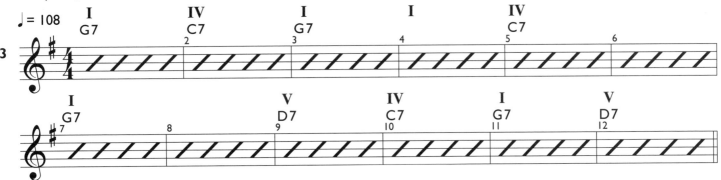

The Dim7 Connector

The following blues uses a diminished 7 chord (dim7). It is similar to the diminished chord we looked at on page 49, except another minor 3rd is added on top. The added note is a ♭7 above the root. The formula for the chord is: root–♭3–♭5–♭7.

In this variation, simply raising the root of the IV chord by one half step creates the dim7 chord; the IV chord (C7) becomes #iv° (C#dim7). The C#dim7 is spelled C# (root), E (♭3), G (♭5) and B♭ (♭7). The diminished 7 chord often makes for an all-purpose transition chord. That is, it will act as a connector chord from one simple chord to another. In this case, it is a great connector from IV back to I.

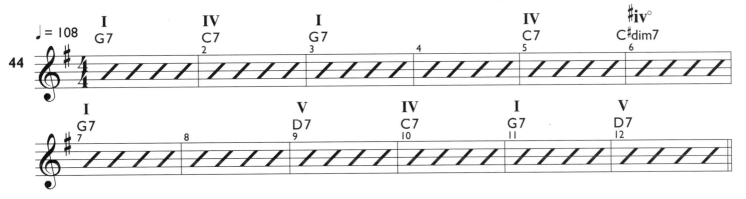

The Cycle of 5ths

Very often, musicians will use the cycle of 5ths to create interesting chord progressions. In the blues, you can approach I, IV or V with chords from outside the key that relate via the cycle of 5ths. For instance, in G, you can approach the V chord (D7) like this: E7–A7–D7. The A7 is not in the key, but it is a 5th above the D7. The E7, which is not in the key either, is a 5th above the A7. Even though E7 and A7 are not in the key, they work because of the cycle of 5ths. Notice that when V (D7) moves to I (G7) the cycle of 5ths is continued.

Take to the Road

"Take to the Road" on the next page uses straight blues changes with a moving bass line in the first chorus. (A *chorus* is a single time through the form of a tune.) In this chorus, you are accompanying (*comping*). Notice the slash chords that appear at the ends of the measures. These quick *passing chords* add a nice twist. In the second chorus, you solo. Between bars 22 and 24, a cycle of 5ths is used to approach the V chord.

Also, this tune uses a *swing eighths* rhythm, which sounds like a triplet with the first two eighth notes tied together. In this book, this rhythm is indicated with the symbol: *Swing 8ths*.

Take to the Road

1st Chorus Comping

Blues Line in the Bass = Rock Power Riffs

When blues riffs are used in the left hand, they can be the basis of some very hot bass lines.

Play the chords indicated in the right hand, and try the left-hand lines in example 45.

To get even more power out of a blues riff, double the notes with the right hand one octave higher. Notice that both hands are playing in bass clef.

Try doubling this bass line with your right hand.

Chapter 10: Funky Sixteenths

Most early rock was based around straight- or swing-eighth notes. They are usually easy to play, read and understand. This chapter deals with sixteenth-note rhythms.

In the late 1960s, and into the 1970s, pop music became more rhythmically complex. Sixteenth-note rhythms became more common. Listeners and dancers, in particular, really liked what sixteenths did to the beat. It added "the funk." Motown and the soul music explosion of the late 1960s moved this style to the forefront of rock and pop music. Rock players were looking for new ways of making *the groove* happen.

Following is a typical bass part using only eighth notes:

Now, there is nothing wrong with the bass line above. It has a strong root feel and moves things along. But suppose it's the last set of the night, the bass player gets a little punchy and holds the first note of the line just one quarter beat too long. This is what happens:

All of a sudden, the bass line starts getting a little loose. The drummer senses what's going on and starts hitting a fat *backbeat* (strong accents on the 2nd and 4th beats). People start dancing like crazy, and a new style of music is born.

Sixteenth notes look more formidable than they really are. All you have to do is divide the beat into four parts instead of two. They are twice as fast as eighth notes. The next example compares eighth notes and sixteenths. For the sixteenth notes, count "1-e-&-ah, 2-e-&-ah, 3-e-&-ah, 4-e-&-ah."

At first, play sixteenth-note passages slowly to ensure accuracy. Check Chapter 12 (page 59) in this book for some sixteenth-note ballads—ballads are slow.

To play repeating sixteenths at a faster tempo, some special techniques can be utilized. The next example shows a way of alternating fingers, right and left, to play rapidly. This method is especially great if you need a rapid, machine-gun-style riff.

Such rapid passages are unusual in rock songs. They are sometimes novelty parts, or a bit of flash to see how quickly the keyboardist can play. More practical are syncopated parts where the keyboardist breaks up the pattern with off-beat accents to make a tune really groove.

Below is a bass line written in two different ways. First, it is written over two measures in eighth notes, then in one measure with sixteenth notes. The two versions will sound identical but in the second version, the beats move twice as slow. This is called *half time*. It takes up half the space and is the way funk lines are usually written.

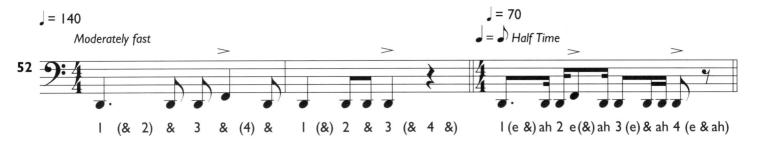

Here is a variation on the bass line from example 52 with variations in the right hand part. Notice the intensive use of syncopation. Syncopation with sixteenths is what funk rhythms are all about.

Track 19 *Explosive Soul*

Chapter 11: In a Modal Mood

The ancient Greeks believed the different modes affected human psychology in particular ways and used them in many ceremonies and celebrations. The Roman Catholic church codified them in the 9th century. Now, they are considered hip scales for rock and jazz improvisation. Nobody in ancient Greece would have laid odds on *that* ever happening!

A *mode* is a reordering of a scale which is then thought of as the *parent scale*. If we play a parent scale starting and ending on something other than the 1st degree, we are playing a mode of the scale. Modes force us to approach harmony in new ways and quite often, the music takes on a unique quality.

Let's take a look at the C Major scale, also called the *Ionian* mode, and how six other modes are derived from it through reordering.

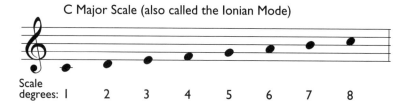

C Major Scale (also called the Ionian Mode)

Scale degrees: 1 2 3 4 5 6 7 8

Modes of the Major Scale

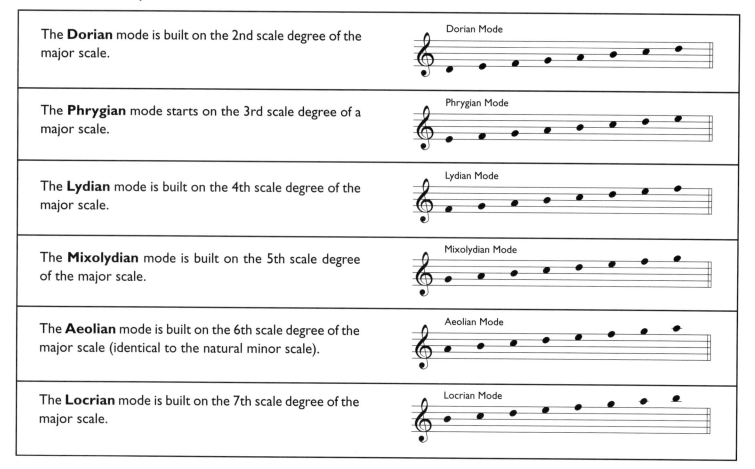

The **Dorian** mode is built on the 2nd scale degree of the major scale.

Dorian Mode

The **Phrygian** mode starts on the 3rd scale degree of a major scale.

Phrygian Mode

The **Lydian** mode is built on the 4th scale degree of the major scale.

Lydian Mode

The **Mixolydian** mode is built on the 5th scale degree of the major scale.

Mixolydian Mode

The **Aeolian** mode is built on the 6th scale degree of the major scale (identical to the natural minor scale).

Aeolian Mode

The **Locrian** mode is built on the 7th scale degree of the major scale.

Locrian Mode

Modes are more often used in contemporary jazz. They are a great alternative to more commonly used scales and add new tones and colors to the music. We will first look into the Dorian and Mixolydian modes since they are the most widely used in rock music. We'll explore the other modes later in the book (see page 100).

The Dorian Mode

The great jam tunes of Santana are among the most famous examples of the Dorian mode in rock music. Below is a Dorian tribute to that group. Lowering the 3rd and 7th of a major scale (♭3 and ♭7) will create a Dorian mode.

The first time through "Pure Magic," play the melody. The second time through, use your right hand to improvise using the D Dorian mode. In the fourth and last repetition, play the written melody again.

Note: Modal pieces use the key signature of the parent scale. So, the key signature for D Dorian is C Major (no sharps or flats).

*Hold last time only

The Mixolydian Mode

The Mixolydian mode is just like the major scale except for the seventh tone, which is a minor 7th (♭7) instead of a major 7th (7). Many bands, such as Phish, have done extended jams in the Mixolydian mode.

"Switch-a-Roo" uses two Mixolydian modes: G Mixolydian and E Mixolydian. The G Mixolydian is used with the G7 chords and the E Mixolydian with the E7 chords. Improvise your own solo in the right hand during the second and third times through the A section.

ff = Fortissimo. Very loud.

Play 3 times

Play 3 times

Chapter 12: Rock Ballads

There comes a time when even the wildest rockers have to show their sensitive sides. Even rockers like Green Day have come up with sensitive ballads such as "Good Riddance (Time of Your Life)," which made their music accessible to a wider audience. Now is the time to put the spotlight on that time-honored tradition: the rock ballad. Yes, it's that time of the night—the slow dance—when you can get romantic with your date.

Let's look back at the styles of the first rock ballads. Following are variations on early rock ballads in the doo-wop style of the 1950s.

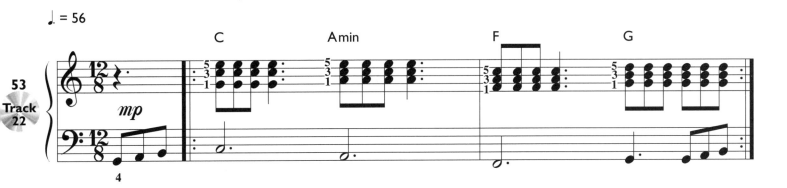

 Roll On

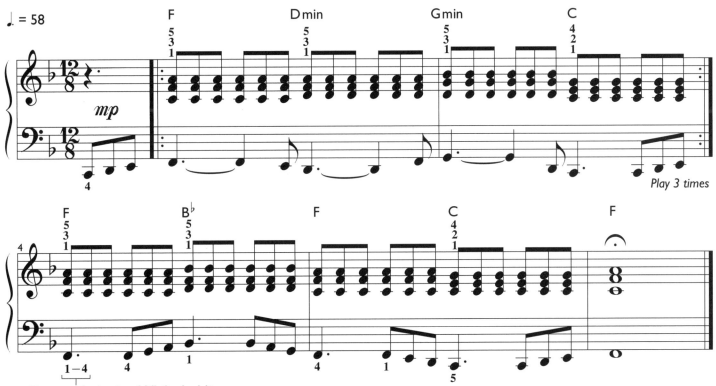

Finger substitution. While holding the key down, switch from the 1st finger to the 4th finger.

Pedal Technique

We haven't used the *sustain pedal* so far in this book. On a standard piano, the right-most pedal is the sustain pedal. Electronic keyboards often come with a single pedal for sustain. In most rock and blues music, the rhythms should be as crisp and hard-edged as possible. In ballads, we can lush it up a bit.

Try the technique. Play a chord and then depress the pedal. Play a second chord. Release the pedal slightly afterwards, so the chords connect but don't ring together for more than an instant. This keeps the chord change clear and clean. Whatever you do, never keep the pedal down all the time. It would muddy the sound considerably.

The following ballad uses sixteenth notes in the right hand. This tune is played very slowly, and the sixteenths should flow smoothly. Notice the use of arpeggios in the intro and coda, and pay special attention to the changing time signatures in the intro.

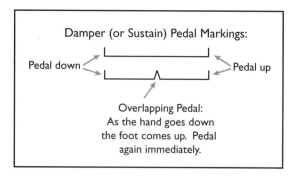

Track 24 *See the Light*

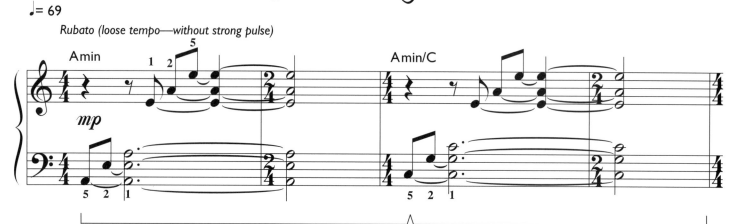

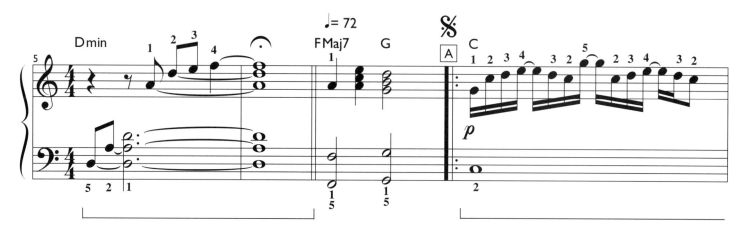

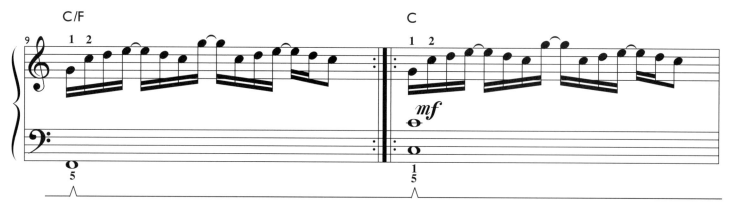

Chapter 13: Electronic Keyboards

Electric Piano

Before the advent of pickups for concert grand pianos and the sampled grand piano, the only way a piano could compete with the roar of a rock band at full tilt was with an electric piano.

The first electric pianos were by the Wurlitzer Company. They had a nicely distorted sound. Ray Charles played one in his hit song "Wha'd I Say" to great effect and the Wurlitzer enjoyed great popularity as a result. It wasn't long before Harold Rhodes invented the Fender Rhodes piano. The Doors used the Fender Rhodes on their album *L. A. Woman*. Since vintage sounds always have an appeal, it is worthwhile to look at the special characteristics of the electric piano.

Generally, electric pianos have fewer keys than a full-size piano. If you have an electric piano sound on your keyboard, try it with the next two tunes. They will sound fine on an acoustic piano but to get the right effect, you should have an electric piano.

In the tune "Lucky," notice the accents in the left hand. When played on the old Wurlitzer-type pianos, they would distort nicely and give the song a great funky sound.

Track 25 *Lucky*

Here's another cool tune to play on the electric piano.

2nd time D.C. al Coda

The Rock Organ: The Mini and the Mighty

The Combo Organ

Similar to the electric piano in size, the combo organ became an integral part of the rock sound in the 1960s. The Doors, Paul Revere and the Raiders, the Dave Clark Five and the Beatles (at Shea Stadium) all used combo organs by companies such as Farfisa, Gibson and Vox.

The sound varies from brand to brand, so there's room for lots of experimentation as you search for similar sounds on your electronic keyboard. One of the nice things about those keyboards is that the output jack is the same quarter-inch phono jack as on a guitar, so guitar effects pedals can be used to alter the sound. Try a distortion or a chorus pedal for a change of tone.

Here are some typical combo organ licks:

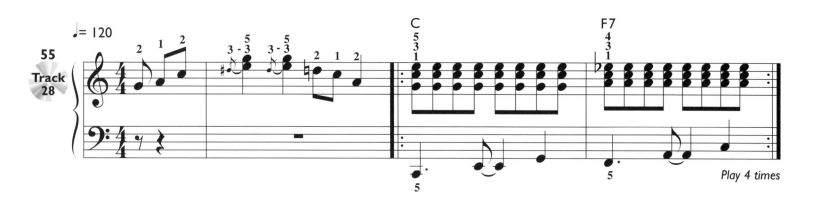

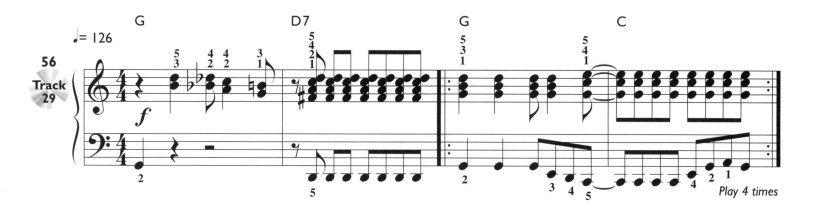

The Mighty Hammond Organ

Hammond organs, particularly the B3 and the C3 models, are classic keyboards whose sounds remain very popular today. The richness of their tones (coming from the old analog "tone generators"), coupled with spinning Leslie speakers, combine to create a unique, heavy texture that is very effective in the rock context.

From the first moment the big chords in the intro hit in this typical Hammond-type tune, the listener knows it's party time! It's in the style of the Spencer Davis Group. Have fun.

Track 30 *Good Time Comin'*

Chapter 14: Important Rock Chords

Power Chords

A *power chord* is a triad with the 3rd omitted, sometimes indicated with a "5," and sometimes with the marking "no 3rd." For example, a power chord on C might be indicated with "C5" or "C no 3rd." In this book, the "5" is used.

Check out the following tune, especially the cool, dark sound of the power chords in the first four measures.

≡ = *Tremolo.* A rapid alternation between two notes. Keep the tremolo going for the value of the notes shown (in this case, the whole note in the sixth measure).

Track 31 *Fingers on Flame*

Sus Chords

A *sus* chord ("sus" is short for "suspended") is a chord where one note, usually the 3rd, has been raised or lowered a step to the next note in the scale. These chords are often (though not always) followed by a *resolution*—the suspended note returning to its proper place. In fact, in traditional classical terms, a suspension is a chord tone held over while the chord changes, thus becoming a non-chord tone that is then resolved. In rock, the term "sus" is more loosely applied. A "proper" resolution is not required. The two most common sus chords found in rock music are the sus4 and the sus2.

Sus4

The *sus4* chord is an altered triad where the 3rd is raised to the 4th tone of the scale. Pete Townsend of the Who makes great use of this chord throughout his rock opera *Tommy*. The movement from the sus4 to the major triad was the basis for much of the piece.

Here are two sus4 chords and their resolutions:

Sus2

The 3rd of a triad can also be lowered to the 2nd tone of the scale becoming a sus2 chord.

Here are two sus2 chords and their resolutions:

Suspended chords can be strung together, going from sus4 to sus2, before returning to a major triad.

7Sus4

A dominant 7th chord can also be suspended with a 4th. This makes for a great build up of harmonic tension before resolving to the tonic chord.

This tune is a great example of how sus chords can be used. Notice the arpeggio texture in the first four and final six bars.

Track 32 *Walk in the Sun*

Major 6 and Major 7 Chords

A *major 6 chord* (Maj6) is comprised of a major triad (root, 3rd and 5th) and an added 6th above the root.

Here is the formula for a C Major 6 chord:

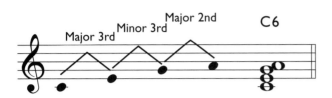

Let's review the major 7 chord. It's similar to the major 6 chord in that it includes a basic major triad, the difference being that it has an added major 7th above the root.

Here is the formula for a C Major 7 chord:

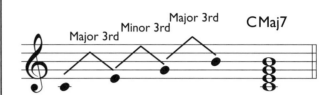

In the example below, you'll learn the Maj6 chord by playing it through the cycle of 5ths. Take your time and get comfortable with each fingering. Also, try to get a feeling for the quality of the sound. If you like, you can play the roots of the chords in your left hand.

Maj6 Chords in the Cycle of 5ths

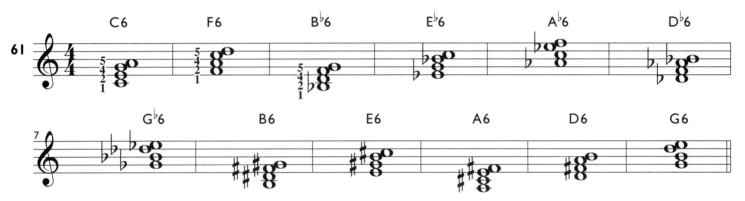

Next, play the same exercise with Maj7 chords. Enjoy the jazzy sound of this harmony and try to think of songs you've heard that include this sound. Again, you can play the roots of the chords in your left hand.

Maj7 Chords in the Cycle of 5ths

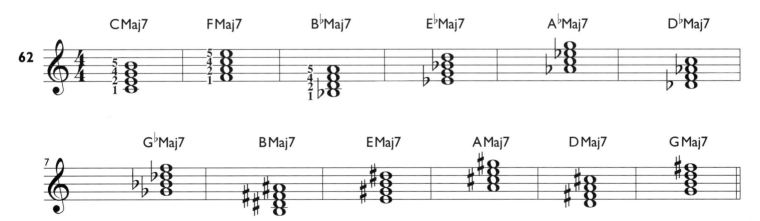

Extensions: Major 9, ♯11 and Major 13

In much the same manner as you created the Maj6 and Maj7 chords, you can add *extensions* to the chords. Extensions are the intervals of a 9th, 11th and 13th. Don't let these fancy sounding numbers throw you. They are really just notes of the major scale in the next higher octave. For instance, the 9th is the 2nd degree of the scale an octave higher. The 11th is the 4th and the 13th is the 6th. Nothing to it! Just remember that the 11th is almost always altered to be a ♯11 so as not to clash with the 3rd. Think of all three of these notes as extensions of the major scale, and they will fit right into your understanding of them as chord extensions.

A major 9 chord (Maj9) is a major triad with an added major 7th and major 9th. Or, look at it this way: from the bottom up, the intervals alternate major 3rd, minor 3rd, major 3rd, minor 3rd.

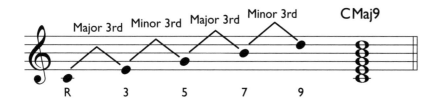

The ♯11 chord will include the major 7th and often the major 9th, as well.

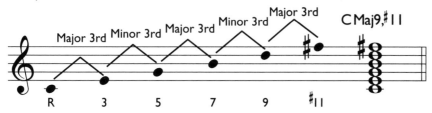

The major 13 chord (Maj13) has the major 7th and often the major 9th. There is another very similar chord called a major 6/9—a major 6 chord with an added 9th. To differentiate the major 13 chord from the 6/9, look for a 7th. If there's a 7th, you have a Maj13 harmony (see note at bottom of page).

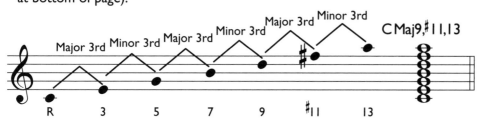

Some players find it helpful to remember this rule: for an extension to work over a chord, the extension must be the interval of a major 9th above the root, 3rd or 5th. Think about it: a ♯11 is a major 9th above the 3rd, a major 13th is a major 9th above the 5th. It works!

> **Note:** A true extension chord always includes the 7th. For example, if a 9th appears above a major triad and no 7th is included, you have an "add9" chord, not a maj9. This may seem picky, but it's an important distinction.

This next tune uses major 9th chords. Be sure to follow the dynamics and accents. When playing five-note chords in one hand, as in the first measure, you can use your thumb to cover two notes. Even though this tune uses lush chords, it should be played at a lively tempo with spirit. Play it slowly at first and increase the tempo as you gain confidence.

Track 33 *No More Clouds*

* Play this chord first time only.

Voicing

The best way to play extended chords is to drop certain notes from the right hand to the left hand. This kind of rearranging of the chord tones between the hands is called *voicing*. Sometimes notes can be left out of a chord. The most common note to be left out is the 5th as shown in the third voicing below. Here are a few examples of how to voice a CMaj9 chord:

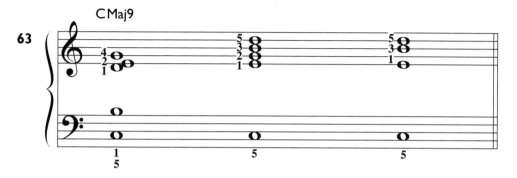

The following tune uses extensions. Notice how they add a spooky, mysterious quality to the harmony. Also, note the swing 8ths indication.

Glow-in-the-Dark

Voice Leading

It is important to be able to use good voice leading between the chords. Voice leading is the art of moving smoothly between chords. Think of each note in a chord as being a "voice," and arrange the notes so that each voice moves smoothly, without large leaps, from one chord to the next. This makes it easier to play since there is less movement required at every chord change. It also sounds great.

Remember that the 3rd and 7th are the most important notes to play in the right hand. They are the notes that lead to other chords. Example 64 shows how the 3rds and 7ths of the chords move to different inversions of chords.

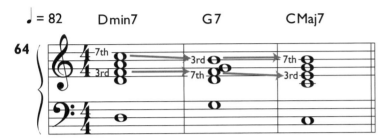

"Time in Motion" demonstrates good voice leading and uses some extensions, too.

Track 35 — *Time in Motion*

*See Note on the bottom of page 70.

Chapter 15: Chord Progressions

A *chord progression* is a succession of chords. Roman numerals are used to understand how the chords relate to each other in a progression and how they all fit into the key. You may want to review the sections on diatonic triads (page 49) and the 12-bar blues (page 50).

I–V–I

One very common rock progression is I–V–I. "Iko Iko," a traditional song first arranged by the Dixie Cups, is comprised of the I–V–I. The Grateful Dead do a great version of this song. A I–V–I progression in the key of C is shown below. Try transposing this progression into every key, using good voice leading.

Below is an example of a I–V–I progression in E. You'll recognize the sound. Notice the root of each chord is in the bass. The notes being played by the right hand include the 3rd and 7th (when present). The tension inherent in the combination of the roots, 3rds and 7ths causes us to want to hear each chord move to the next. After hearing the I chord and then V, your ear wants to hear the I chord again.

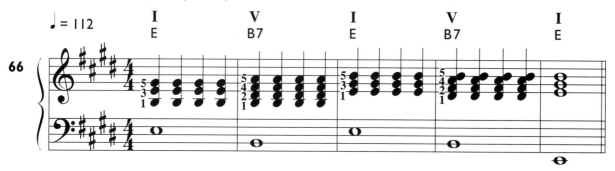

I–IV–V–IV and V–IV–I

Two very common rock 'n' roll chord progressions are I–IV–V–IV and V–IV–I. They are both found in numerous songs. Below is an example of the I–IV–V–IV.

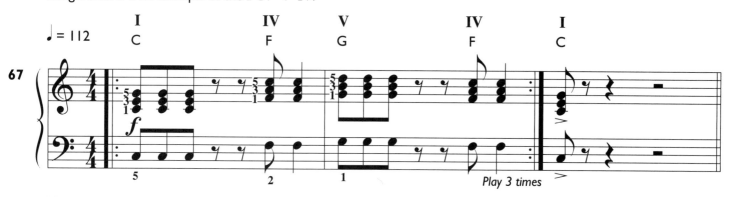

Here is an example of the V–IV–I progression:

One of the most popular rock progressions is V–IV–I. There are hundreds of rock tunes that use this progression. Check out the John Hiatt tune "Sure Pinocchio." Here is a tune in the style of John Hiatt using this important chord progression. Pay attention to the key signature. This song is in E—a very common rock 'n' roll key.

Track 36 *Go Geppetto*

Probably the most famous example of the I–IV–V–IV progression is the Kingsman's timeless hit "Louie, Louie." Another great example is "Summer Nights" from the Broadway show *Grease*. Here's a tune for you to play using this progression.

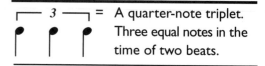

A quarter-note triplet. Three equal notes in the time of two beats.

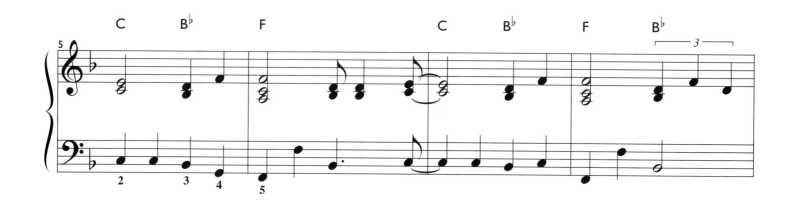

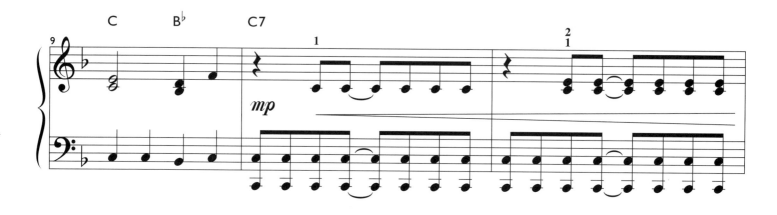

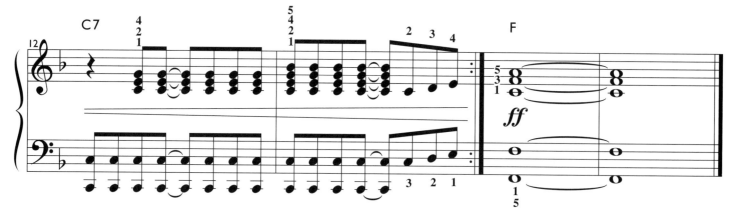

Why I–IV–V–I Rules Rock'n' Roll

I, IV and V are the most important chords in rock music, known as the *primary chords*. It's worth understanding why that is true, because we will find that the relationships between these chords affect many chord progressions.

Our ears are accustomed to hearing chords move in a downward (counterclockwise) cycle of 5ths. For that reason, a song starting on a I chord—as most rock songs do—will tend to move downward by a 5th to the IV chord. In the key of C, we start on a C chord and move to an F chord.

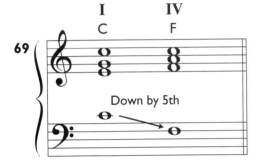

Think of the I chord as being like a magnetized home base. Imagine that, like a magnet, it draws the chords in the progression back to itself. So, now that the progression has moved to IV, the progression strives to move back to I. The quickest route back to I is the V7 chord. There are three reasons for this:

1. We want to hear movement downward by 5th, and the movement from V7 to I is downward by 5th.

2. The 3rd of the V7 chord is the *leading tone* in the key—the 7th note of the major scale. That note is very powerfully drawn to the root (1 or 8 of the scale, the root of the I chord). Try playing a C Major scale stopping on B, the 7th note. It's a very unsatisfying sound. You will want to hear that note move up to the eighth note of the scale, C.

3. The 7th of the V7 chord sounds like it wants to fall a half step to the 3rd of the I chord. You'll hear this when you play the following example.

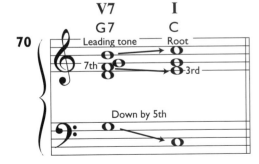

When you take all of this into consideration, it's no wonder the I–IV–V–I progression is so common and so important.

Substitutions for I–IV–V–I

Obviously, if we only used the primary chords in every song, music would soon become boring. Yes, even rock music would collapse under the weight of boredom. Thankfully, there are some easy ways to vary the I–IV–V progression by substituting chords that are similar.

Each of the primary chords shares notes in common with several other chords. For instance, the IV chord shares three notes with ii (min7). This chord can be substituted for IV.

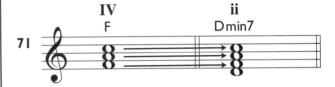

Some other good examples of this can be found when considering the V chord (example 72A), which shares three notes with both the iii (min7) and the vii (min7♭5). Either of these chords can be substituted for V. Even the I chord can be replaced with a substitution.

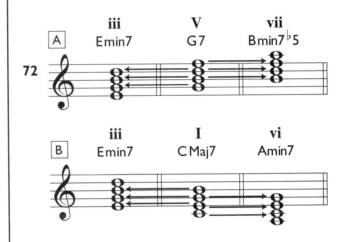

Through combinations of these chord substitutions, we can create a variety of different chord progressions. Let's examine some possibilities.

The first line in the example below shows a basic I–IV–V–I progression in E. (You need to get used to this key—guitarists love it.) It is followed by three variations on the progression. It's exciting to realize just how creative you can be and still make progressions that work because they are based on I–IV–V–I. The chords being replaced with substitutions are shown in parentheses.

I–vi–IV–V

The I–vi–IV–V is a classic progression. Many hit songs from the 1950s and early 1960s have this progression, including "Earth Angel" (recorded by the Penguins and the Crew-Cuts), "Sixteen Candles" (the Crests) and "Heart and Soul." Let's have some fun with this one. Note the $\frac{6}{8}$ time signature. Think of it as having two beats per measure, with the dotted quarter note equaling one beat.

Track 38 *Sixteen Angels*

A Mixolydian Chord Progression (the ♭VII)

If you compare the Mixolydian mode to the major scale, you will notice that the 7th note in the Mixolydian mode is one half step lower. If you harmonize the Mixolydian mode diatonically, just as we did with the major scale (see page 49), the chord built on the ♭7 (♭VII) is a major triad.

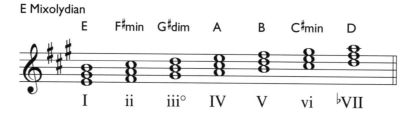

A common Mixolydian progression in rock music is the I–♭VII–IV progression. "Gloria" by Van Morrison is a great example of a song with this progression, as is "Mississippi Moon" by King's X. Here's a tune for you to play with the I–♭VII–IV progression.

Here's a tune that incorporates many ideas from this chapter. A *harmonic analysis,* or analysis of the chord progression, is included (gray Roman numerals).

Chapter 16: Diatonic Soloing

In the Diatonic Triads section (page 49), you learned how to formulate chords from the notes of the major scale, and that these chords are assigned Roman numerals that help us relate them to the key. This information is also important for improvising solos.

Diatonic 7th Chords

When thinking diatonically, there is one chord in particular that helps to establish the key: the V7 chord. This is because there is only one dominant 7th chord (a major triad with a minor 7 above the root—see page 23) in any key. In the key of C, that chord is G7. Here are the diatonic 7th chords—the 7th chords that are built on each note of the major scale:

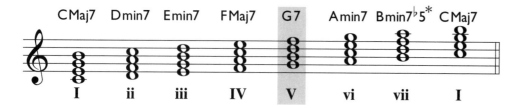

* The minor 7 flat 5 chord may be new to you. It's a diminished triad, 1–♭3–♭5—stacked minor 3rds—with a major 3rd (♭7) stacked on top.

The cool thing about the V7 chord is that it wants to resolve to a I chord of some kind. If you review example 70 on page 77, you will recall some reasons why V7 gravitates towards I. Another reason for this tendency is the inherent tension in the dominant 7th chord. This is due to the interval of a tritone (♯4 or ♭5) formed by the 3rd and 7th. A tritone is a dissonant interval. Look at the diagram to the right to see the interval of a tritone in the V7 chord and how it resolves to the consonant major 3rd in the I chord.

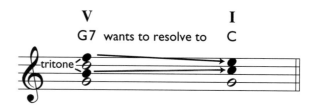

Play the example above and you will hear how "right" the resolution sounds. This sound helps to establish the key of C. It's like a sign by the side of the road that says "Now Entering the Key of C." When you are looking at any tune, a good understanding of diatonic harmony will help you see the V7 chord and find its resolution to I. This will make it easier to determine the key, which makes it very easy to solo. After all, if all the chords are in C, you can just rock out on a C Major scale! Play it fast, play it slow, play the notes in any order, vary the rhythms—improvise.

Analyzing a Song

To improvise on a tune, you must first understand all the chords and know what key they are in. This is so that you can choose an appropriate scale(s) to use. Recognizing the V7 to I in a progression, as discussed on page 82, is an important first step. Study the diatonic 7th chords on page 82 and note that the diatonic chords in a key always follow the chart to the right.

Chord	Triad	7th Chords
I	major	major 7
ii	minor	minor 7
iii	minor	minor 7
IV	major	major 7
V	major	dominant 7
vi	minor	minor 7
vii	diminished	minor 7♭5

Let's try some analysis. Look at the chords in example 77. It starts with a Gmin7. You know that in any key, a minor 7 chord can be a ii chord, iii chord or vi chord. Look at the next chord. It is a C7 chord. You know that the only diatonic dominant 7 chord is V. To determine the key in which C7 is V, count to five backwards through the alphabet from C (C, B, A, G, F). C would be the V chord in F. In example 77, the chord after the C7 chord is an FMaj7 chord; so, you can assume that the Gmin7 is a ii chord in F and that the C7 is V. You can play an F Major scale over all of those chords.

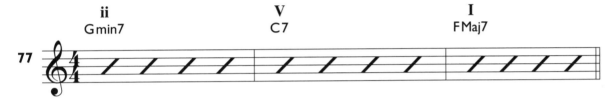

Imagine you are given a chart for the chord progression below. Try your hand at an analysis. Use a pencil and write Roman numerals above the staff. Remember, it is okay to skip chords and work your way backwards if it is easier. Turn the page upside down to check your work.

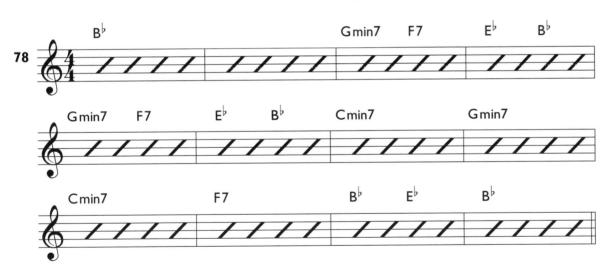

Answers to example 78. Turn upside down to read.

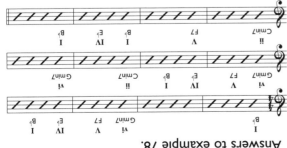

Applying the Major Scale to a Solo

You should have figured out that example 78 on page 83 is in the key of B♭. You can play a B♭ Major scale over the entire example. Using the same example, try playing the chords in your left hand and the scale in your right. Listen to how it sounds. Then, try starting the scale on the root of each chord. The following example demonstrates this technique.

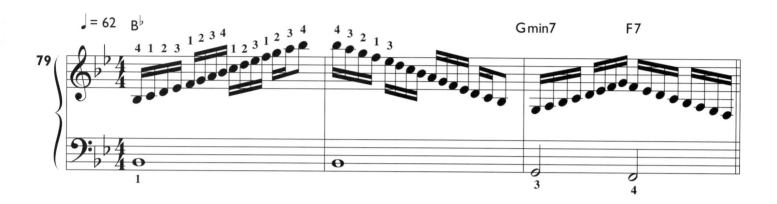

Another technique is to outline the chords with arpeggios. Arpeggios are cool because they are a good way of moving your hand from one octave to another. You can arpeggiate a chord in any inversion. Since the chords are diatonic, we are just arranging the notes of the major scale into arpeggios.

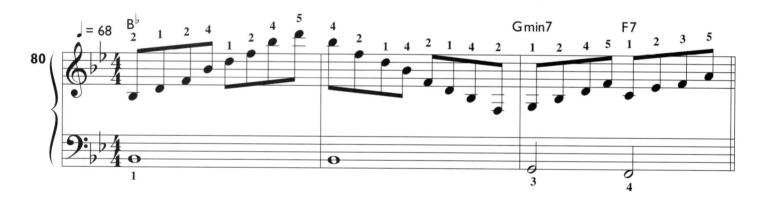

"Oolong Tea" further illustrates arpeggiation in a solo
and movement through octaves.

Track
41   *Oolong Tea*

Phrasing, Chord Tones and Passing Tones

To be a great player, you must learn to listen and phrase ideas melodically and rhythmically. A good player learns when to play a lot and when to be quiet. Think of the way horn players play when soloing. They breathe between ideas; they have to. This creates space which can add to a solo. You also want to build a solo to a climax, or a few climaxes, that will get the other band members and the audience excited.

A good way of creating melodic, rhythmic and nicely phrased solos is to think in terms of *chord tones* and *passing tones*. Chord tones are the notes that make up the chord (root, 3rd, 5th, 7th, etc.). In rock music, passing tones are notes that aren't part of the chord but are part of the key that the chord is in. Some notes that rock musicians think of as "passing tones" are sometimes given other names by classical musicians, such as "auxiliary tones" or "neighbor tones." While we sometimes use terms like these, most often we put all of these tones in the broad category of passing tones. These notes usually lead to a chord tone. The next tune is an example of a solo that uses phrased lines incorporating arpeggios, passing tones and chord tones.

Track 42 — *Oolong Groove*

♩ = Passing tone
*

Below is a solo for you to play. Learn to play the solo shown, then try improvising your own right-hand solo over the existing left-hand part. Notice the grace note in measure 3. Quickly slide your 2nd finger off the D♯ and on to the E.

Track 43 *Point of View*

Harmonizing Your Lines

Sometimes, single notes in a solo can get a bit dull. Playing in 3rds or in 6ths is a cool way to add texture to your sound and variety to your improvisations.

The example below shows the intervals of a 3rd and a 6th:

Notice what happens if you invert these intervals. They invert into each other! In other words, if you invert a 3rd, it becomes a 6th. The 6th inverts to a 3rd. Also, the quality of the interval changes, so a major interval inverted is minor, and a minor interval inverted is major.

Once you have analyzed and figured out what key you are in, you can harmonize your solo with 3rds and 6ths. Check out the following example.

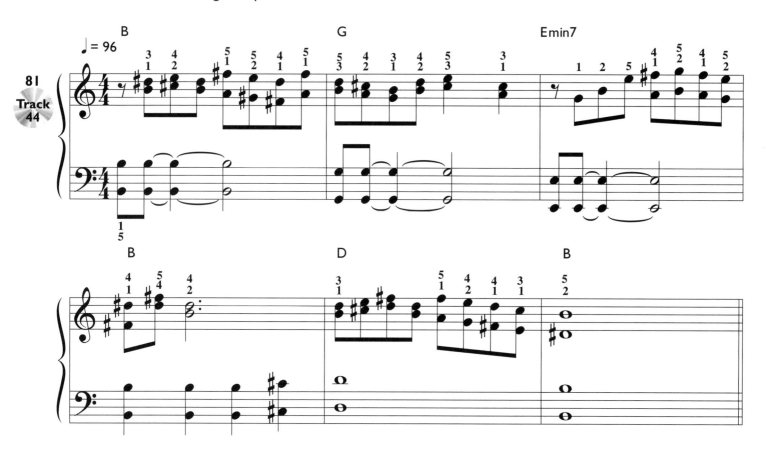

Billy Joel's "Streetlife Serenader" is a good example of a song that uses this technique. It is loaded with chordal patterns, but the top notes in the chords are 3rds and 6ths. Also, listen to "Let It Be" by the Beatles. The introduction is a line harmonized in 3rds.

"Streetsweeping Troubadour" is in the style of Billy Joel. The rhythm isn't as tough as it looks! Just count carefully, subdividing by sixteenth notes where necessary (1-e-&-ah, 2-e-&-ah, etc.).

Streetsweeping Troubadour

Licks and Tricks

A *lick* is a short melodic line. Some licks are so commonly used that they have become a part of our universal musical language. Over time, a good musician will memorize hundreds of licks and use them in solos. Remember that these licks are used in conjunction with—not instead of—improvisation. Hopefully, you will constantly be inventing new licks of your own.

Below are a few licks to learn. Try each of them in every key. This first one demonstrates how a little repetition can be a good thing:

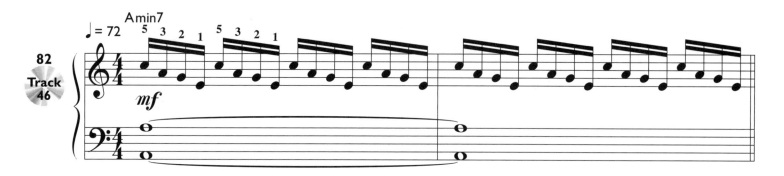

Example 83 is a triplet idea.

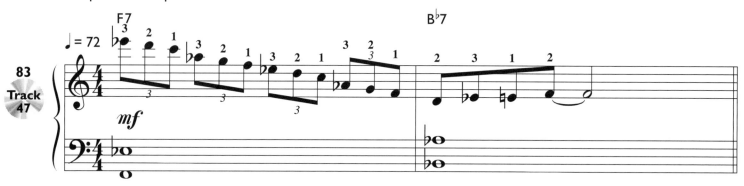

Count the sixteenth-note rhythms in examples 84 and 85 carefully.

The lick in example 86 shows how a single idea, in this case the interval of a descending 3rd, can be used to build a great lick. The descending interval is repeated numerous times, starting on a different note each time. This is called a *sequence*.

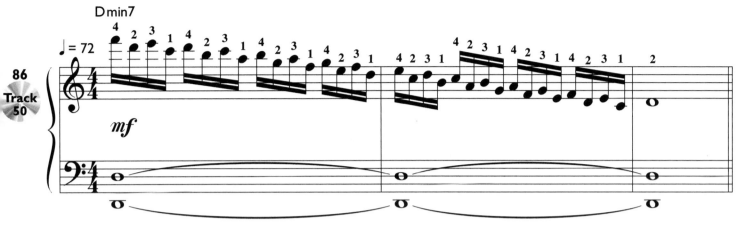

In example 87, chords are outlined with arpeggios to create the lick.

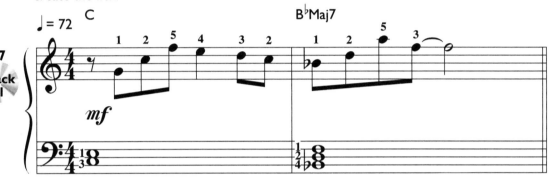

Example 88 uses *neighbor tones* (non-chord tones a step above or below a chord tone that return to the chord tone—in this case the D♯) to create interest. Also, note the syncopated rhythms.

In example 89, the line is in the top note of each chord. Playing a chord under each note in a line is a great way to give it added weight and volume.

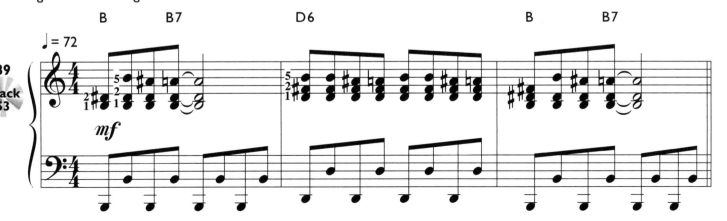

The following tune shows how licks can be put together
to make a solo.

195 Relics

♩ = 68

Chapter 17: Minor Chord Extensions

Minor 9, 11 and 13 Chords

In Chapter 14, you began your study of chord extensions with 9ths, 11ths and 13ths. Let's continue your progress towards good rock chordsmanship and learn about the minor extensions: the minor 9 (min9), minor 11 (min11) and minor 13 (min13) chords. As with the major extensions, minor extensions are the interval of a major 9th above the root, 3rd and/or 5th of the chord. Also, remember that extended chords always include the 7th (see note at the bottom of page 70).

A minor 9 chord is a minor triad with an added ♭7 and major 9th. Or, look at it this way: from the bottom up, the intervals alternate minor 3rd, major 3rd, minor 3rd, major 3rd.

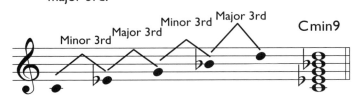

The minor 11 chord will include the ♭7 and the 9th. Notice that the intervals continue to alternate, minor, major, minor, major, etc.

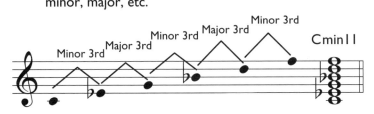

You get the idea—we just continue to stack 3rds to create further extensions of the original triad. For the minor 13 chord, stack an additional major 3rd on top of the min11 chord.

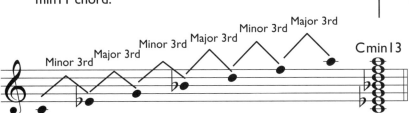

Voicing Minor Extensions

You can use various voicings for the minor extensions. It is important to remember that it is okay to leave out the 5th of the chord. You can play the basic chord tones in the left hand and the extensions, in any order, in the right hand. Study the following examples and try to create some voicings of your own.

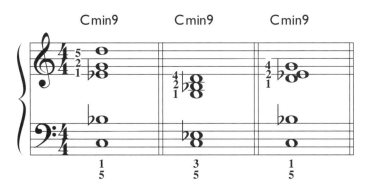

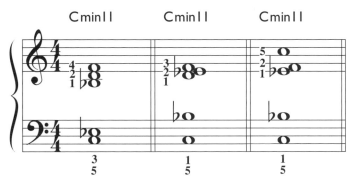

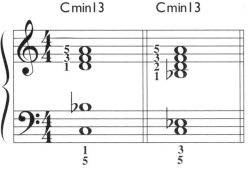

"Madman's Minors" uses the lush sounds of voiced
minor extensions.

Madman's Minors

Track 55

Chapter 18: Developing Bass Lines

Rock music always needs a solid foundation in the bass. As the keyboard player, you may sometimes be called upon to fill in for a bass player with your left hand, and it's not unusual to double the bass line (play along with the bass player). In Chapter 5, we looked at some easy bass lines. Let's continue by revisiting the most basic, and one of the coolest, types of bass lines—the pedal tone.

More Pedal Tones

A pedal tone is a note, usually in the bass, that is repeated or sustained as chords change. Most often, it is a note that is sustained through many measures. This is something that is used to create tension or excitement in a song. Slash chord symbols are the most common way of expressing this idea in a lead sheet (for example, G/C—G is the chord, C is in the bass). Play examples 90 and 91 and notice how the tension builds as the bass note is repeated while the chords change.

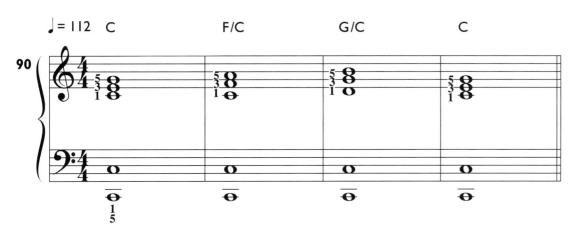

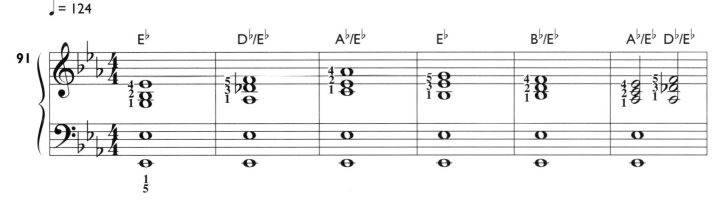

Here's a fun tune to play using pedal tones.

Track 56 *Rolls Like a Wave*

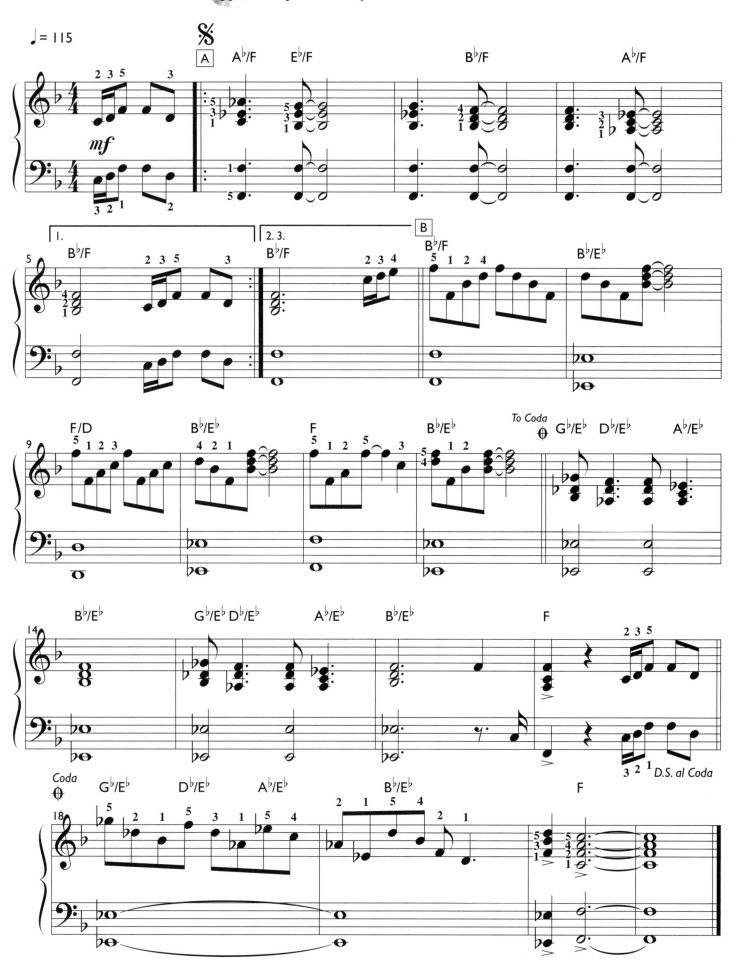

Walking Bass

Walking bass is a style of bass line that outlines a chord progression using primarily quarter notes. As a general rule, it's best to play the root of the chord on the downbeat of each measure. On the other beats, you can choose either a chord tone or a passing tone (see page 86). Carefully selected passing tones will give your bass line a smooth, jazzy sound.

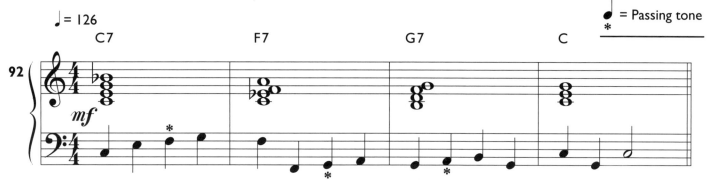

The example above is fairly basic and will work in many styles of rock music. If you are playing in a band with a strong jazz influence, you can probably get away with more adventurous bass lines. Let your ear be your guide and select notes that make the whole band sound good. The following example is a 12-bar blues with some advanced walking bass techniques, including *chromatic passing tones* (measures 3, 5 and 9) and *chromatic approach tones* (measures 4, 6, 11 and 12). Chromatic passing tones are non-diatonic tones in between two consecutive scale tones. Chromatic approach tones are notes that approach a scale tone from one half step above or below. Both of these types of notes are outside the key or current chord and move by half step to the next chord tone. This bass line also uses *rhythmic variation* (measures 2, 4, 6, 8 and 10) to spice up the quarter-note pulse.

The Falling Bass

The falling bass is a less jazz/blues-flavored version of the walking bass. Using passing tones and/or chord inversions, indicated with slash chords, songwriters will often write lines that descend in a stepwise manner, usually landing on chord tones on the downbeats. Billy Joel's "Piano Man" is a song that illustrates this well, as is "Dear Prudence" by the Beatles. The following tune will give you an introduction to the falling bass.

Probably the most famous example of a falling bass line in a rock tune is "A Whiter Shade of Pale" by Procol Harum. The bass line is simply a descending major scale harmonized diatonically with chords in root position and inversion. The line and progression of the song were actually taken from "Air on a G String," a piece from an orchestral suite by Johann Sebastian Bach (1685–1750). "Going for Baroque" on page 99 is in the style of this classic tune.

Note: Measure 16 of "Going for Baroque" on the next page includes a long *gliss*. A gliss is a rapid scale passage performed by sliding the hand(s) or fingers over the keys. This particular gliss starts on a high G (two octaves and a 5th above middle C), goes down to a low G (a 4th below middle C) and back up again.

Gliss Down and Up

Going for Baroque

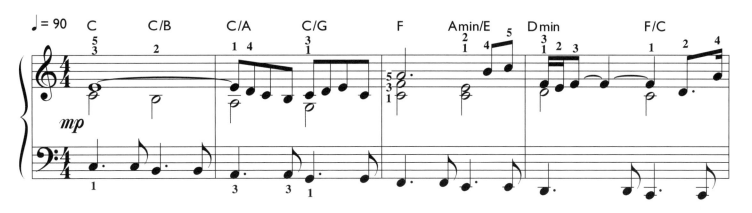

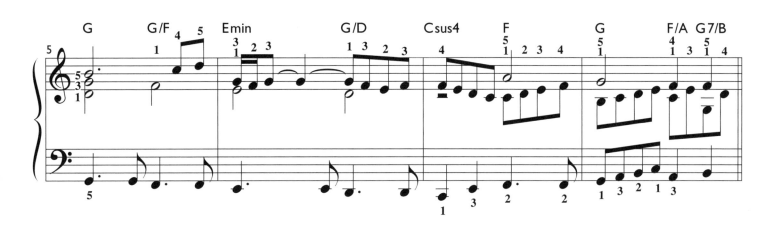

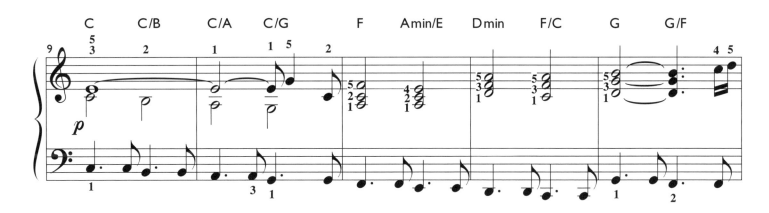

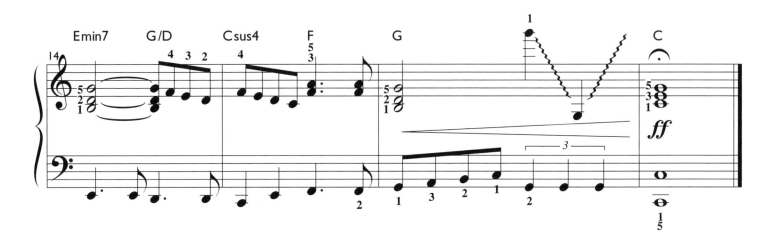

Chapter 19: More Scales and Modes

As you learned earlier (page 56), a mode is a reordering of a scale which is then thought of as the parent scale. If you play a parent scale starting and ending on something other than the 1st degree, you are playing a mode of the scale. Through each mode's characteristic sound, you can create interesting chord progressions and melodies. We already looked at the Dorian and Mixolydian modes. Now, let's look at the Phrygian, Lydian and Aeolian modes.

Phrygian

Phrygian is the mode based on the 3rd degree of the major scale. The Phrygian mode is commonly associated with heavy metal, but it is also common in Spanish music. Flamenco guitarists play this mode often; some people think of it as "the bull fighting" mode.

Here is the Phrygian mode on E:

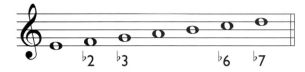

Note that this mode can be created by lowering the 2nd, 3rd, 6th and 7th of a major scale ($\flat$2, $\flat$3, $\flat$6 and $\flat$7). These alterations create the Mediterranean sound of the mode.

You can also create diatonic chords for the Phrygian mode, just as for the major scale. Songs are sometimes based on chords from the Phrygian mode, and being able to identify such chord progressions will help you know when to use the mode in your improvisations.

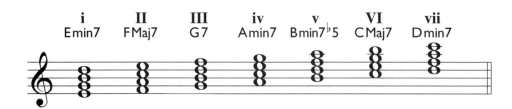

Notice that just as the notes of the C Major scale have been reordered to create the E Phrygian mode, the diatonic chords have been reordered. For example, in C Major, the E Minor triad is iii; in E Phrygian it's i. The most distinctive feature of this mode is the half-step relationship between the minor i and the major II.

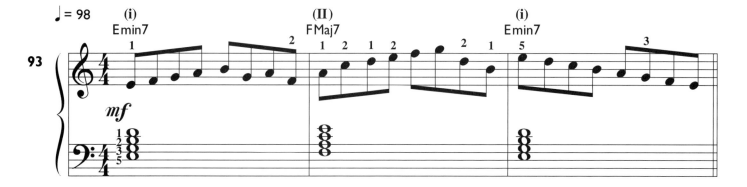

Remember that modal pieces use the key signature of
the parent scale. So, the key signature for E Phrygian is C
Major (no sharps or flats). Enjoy playing this tune in the
Phrygian mode.

Wagons to Phrygia

Track
60

* N.C. means no chord.

Lydian

The Lydian mode has a very unusual and interesting sound. Built on the 4th degree of the parent major scale, Lydian has a ♯4.

Here is the Lydian mode on F:

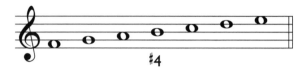

Below are the diatonic chords for the Lydian mode on F. Remember that this is merely a reordering of the diatonic chords of the parent scale, C Major. What was once IV in C Major is now I in F Lydian.

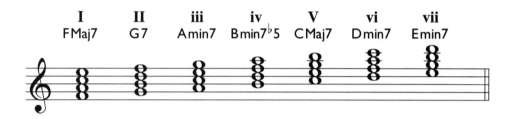

The most notable characteristic of this mode is the ♯4 (in F Lydian—the B), so be sure to give that tone emphasis in your Lydian solos. Here is an example of a Lydian chord progression and melody:

Here's a tune in C Lydian. The parent scale is G Major and
the #4 is F#. Watch for the $\frac{2}{4}$ time change in measure 17.

Track 62 — Lydian Mood

Aeolian

The Aeolian mode is built on the 6th degree of the major scale. It is also known as the natural minor or the relative minor scale of its parent major scale (see page 17). This mode can also be created by lowering the 3rd, 6th and 7th of a major scale (♭3, ♭6 and ♭7).

Here is the Aeolian scale on A:

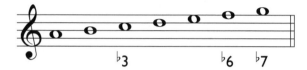

Here are the diatonic chords for the Aeolian mode:

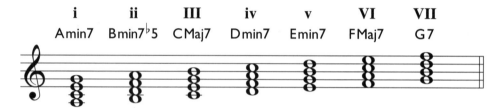

The Aeolian mode is the relative minor of its parent major scale, C Major. You can think of it as the "minor side" of the major key. Here's a short example of the Aeolian mode in A.

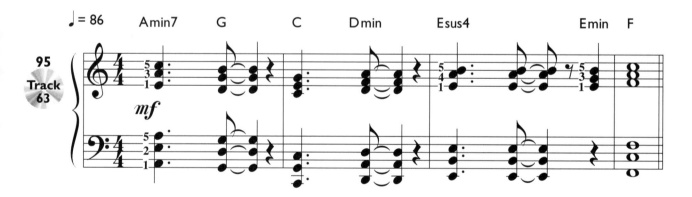

Here's a tune in A Aeolian. Enjoy!

8va----- = *All'ottava bassa.* Play the bracketed notes one octave lower than written.

Track 64 *Galaxy of Love*

♩ = 105

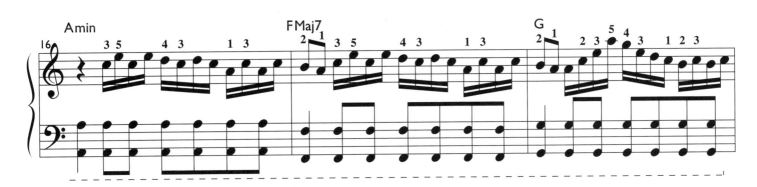

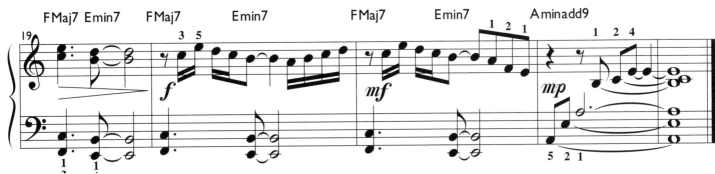

Harmonic Minor

This scale is used in lots of metal tunes. Artists such as Yngwie Malmsteen use it for improvisation, and Aerosmith's "Taste of India" uses harmonic minor sounds as well. The harmonic minor scale is built by raising the 7th degree of the natural minor scale (Aeolian mode). It can also be created by lowering the 3rd and 6th degrees of a major scale (♭3 and ♭6). The characteristic feature of this scale is the augmented 2nd (one whole step plus a half step) between the ♭6 and 7 of the scale. This scale has the exotic sound of snake charming music. Get out your magic carpet!

Here is a harmonic minor scale on C:

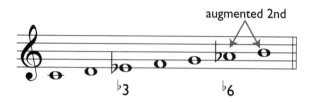

Below are the diatonic chords for the harmonic minor scale in C. Notice the dramatic effect the 7th degree has on the chords. Remember, the harmonic minor scale can be thought of as an Aeolian mode with the 7th raised. In the Aeolian mode, the ♭7 fits right into standard diatonic harmony and the chords are simply reordered from the parent major scale. In the harmonic minor, the harmonies are quite different. The i chord is a minor triad with a major 7th, written min(Maj7). Also, note the III chord. It's an augmented triad with a major 7th, written Maj7♯5. These unusual harmonies add to the exotic quality of the mode.

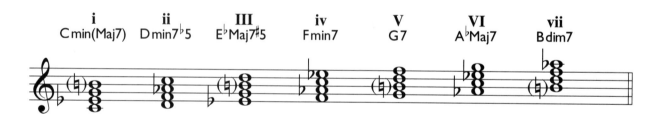

This scale works great over any ii–V progression where ii is a min7♭5 and V is 7♭9. Remember, ii is a great substitute for IV in the mighty I–IV–V–I progression. For example, if you see Dmin7♭5 (D–F–A♭–C) going to a G7♭9 (G–B–D–F–A♭), you can improvise with the C Harmonic Minor scale. Check out measures 2, 4 and 7 of "Harmonic Detective" on page 107 to see how the scale works in this situation.

Enjoy the exotic harmonic minor sound of "Harmonic Detective." Remember, in $\frac{12}{8}$ time, there are four beats per measure and the dotted quarter note equals one beat.

Harmonic Detective

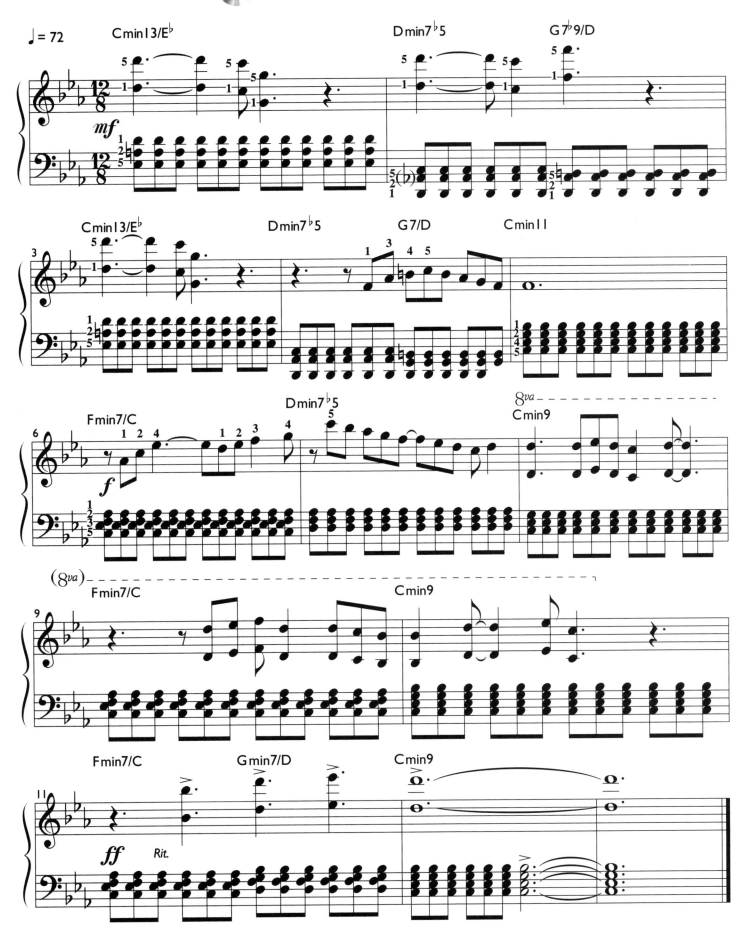

Chapter 20: Styles

To become a versatile musician, and to develop a truly unique personal style, it is first necessary to study the styles of others. This will provide a point of departure for your own growth. This chapter will investigate a variety of important rock styles.

In the Style of Pink Floyd

Pink Floyd, the premier psychedelic group of the 1970s, is still around playing haunting melodies and wonderful, rich chords. For Pink Floyd, creating interesting textures has always been the goal. Even though they are known for their spacey sounds, they can also rock hard. This next tune is in the style of "Run Like Hell" from their masterpiece, *The Wall*. It uses staccato bass lines with chords that slice like a knife. Play it with maximum spirit!

Track 66 *Full Moon Frenzy*

(Continue L.H. an octave lower)

In the Style of Steely Dan

Steely Dan created their own style of rock 'n' roll and quickly became very popular in the 1980s. They incorporated rich harmonies and interesting chord progressions borrowed from jazz. Check out the songs "Deacon Blues" and "Peg" to hear their distinctive approach to chords and progressions. "Blue Mercedes" is in the style of Steely Dan. If you have a synth, try an electric piano sound. Or, even better, dust off your Fender Rhodes and go to town! On the CD, the entire song is played twice.

Track 67 *Blue Mercedes*

Blues Rock

The music of the Allman Brothers, the Grateful Dead, the Black Crowes, Jonny Lang and Kenny Wayne Shepherd are just a few great examples of this style. Guitars are featured prominently in these groups, but often vintage keyboards, such as the Hammond organ or a honky tonk piano, are used for solos and backing parts. Using blues chord changes and scales (pentatonic), these artists clearly demonstrate the blues roots of rock music. Here is a tune in the style of the Grateful Dead. On the CD, the song is played through four times. The second and third times through, only the chords are played, so you can try soloing over the changes.

Track 68 *Evenin' Dew*

Chapter 21: More Soloing and Harmonic Theory

Solo Examples

Soloing encompasses any situation where an instrument is featured. This could be anything from playing a solo piano piece to playing a featured part within an ensemble.

Following are some examples of possible solos. Hopefully, they will provide you with ideas to build on for your own solos.

This solo is a rock ballad for piano. It is not very technical, focusing mostly on the melodic material. A good solo doesn't need to be flashy!

Track 69 *All I Need*

Λ = *Marcato.* Play with even more attack than a regular accent.

This solo is more technically advanced, mainly featuring arpeggios in the right hand. Practice slowly at first and build up to the suggested tempo. Notice the *sextuplets*, six notes played in the time of four of the same value (in this case, six sixteenth notes in the time of four—one beat).

In Search of the Broken Chord

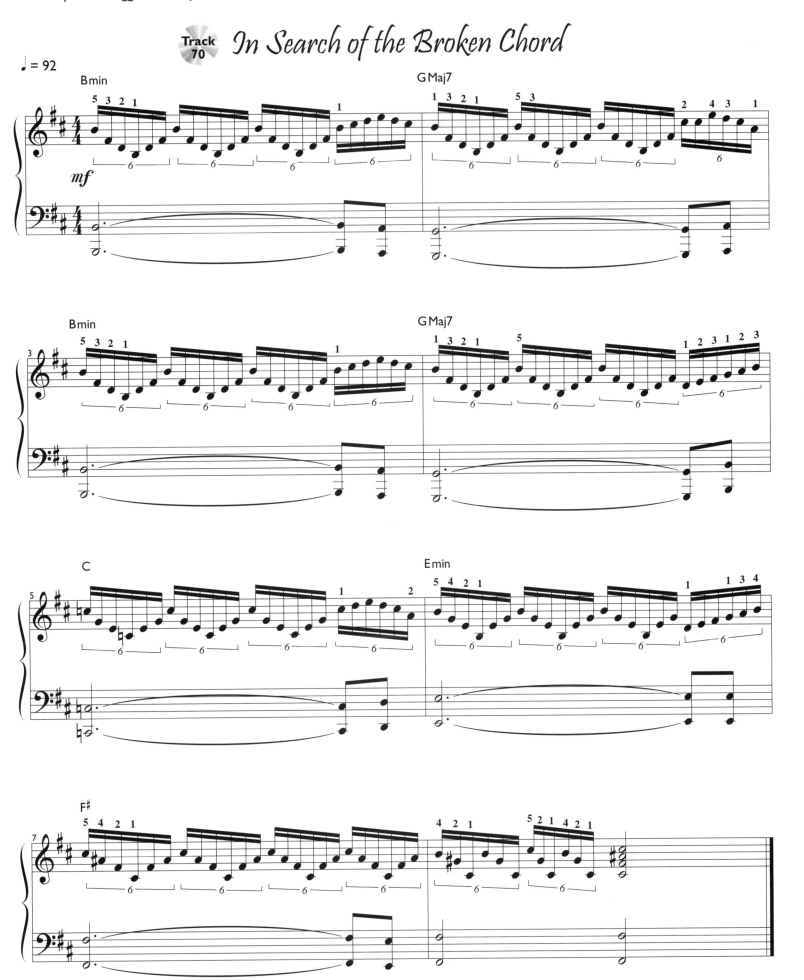

This solo is fairly technically advanced, but demonstrates that a flashy solo can be melodic too. Pay attention to the accent marks, and the melodic content will be clearer.

Track 71 *Technically Tuneful*

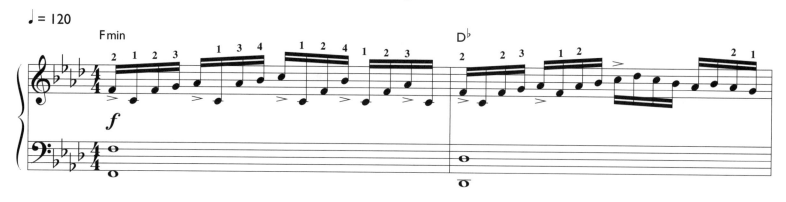

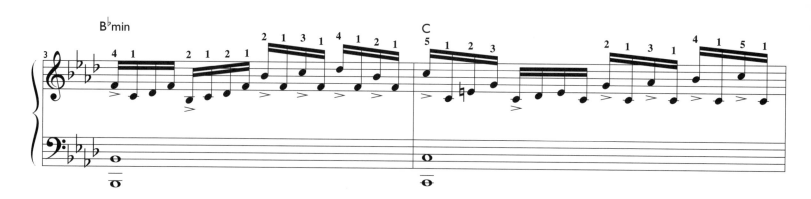

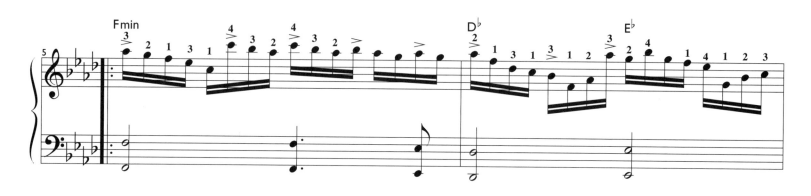

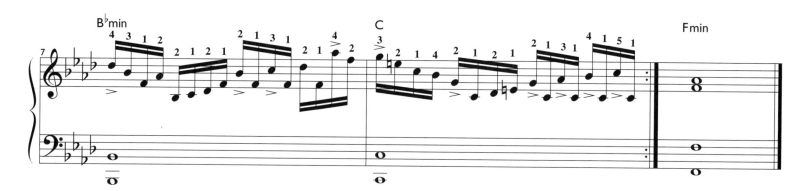

"Serendipity" is a progressive rock keyboard solo. Play it with a Minimoog sound. Be expressive. Don't just read the notes. Practice slowly at first. This one will take a while to perfect. It's unlikely that a keyboard player would ever have to accommpany a solo like this with their left hand, so only a right-hand part is shown.

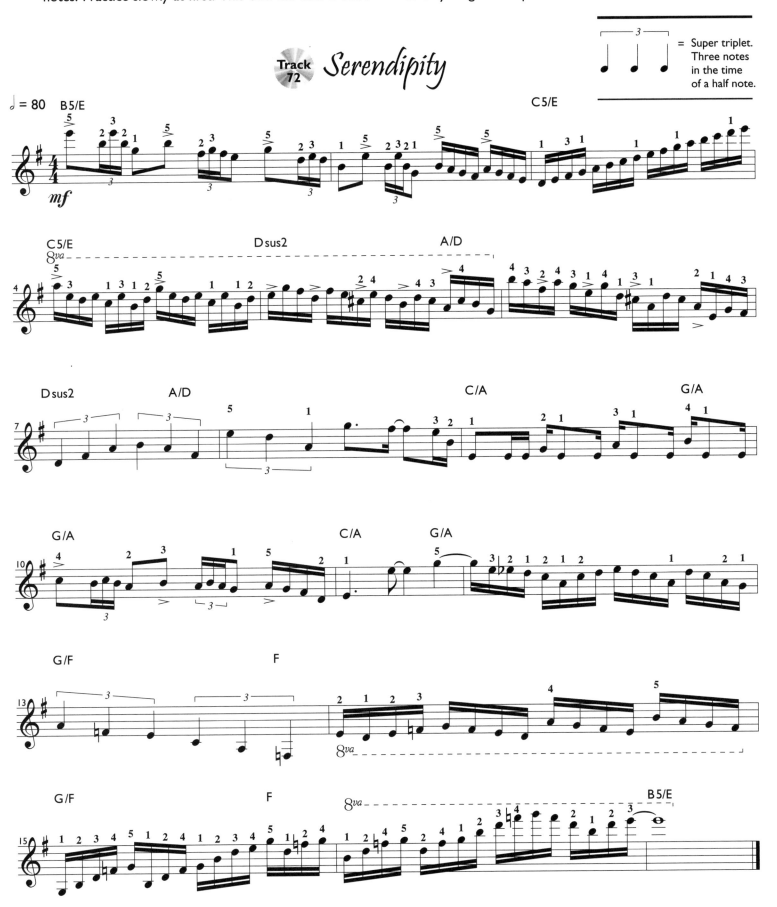

Exercise: Hopefully, these pieces have gotten your creative juices flowing. Try to compose a solo of your own in each style demonstrated in this chapter.

Relating Diatonic Harmonization to the Modes

Diatonic harmonization of the major scale is based on *tertiary* (ter-shi-ar-e: characterized by or based on the number three) harmony. The various degrees of the scale are harmonized in 3rds, thus creating triads and 7th chords. Since the modes of the major scale are all strictly diatonic—that is, they are merely a re-ordering of the major scale—the harmonies derived from the scale can be modal as well.

Here is a quick review, showing the C Major scale and its diatonic 7th chords. We can call this the *C Major chord scale*. The corresponding modes are listed under the chord scale.

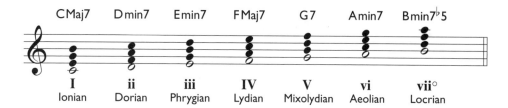

Each chord in the major chord scale can be thought of as characterizing a particular mode of the scale. For example, if we want to improvise over a min7 chord, our choices are narrowed down to three possible modes—Dorian, Phrygian and Aeolian—because these are the only three modes that contain the notes of a min7 chord (1–♭3–5–♭7). You can use any one of these three modes to solo over a min7 chord.

Now, if we play a *vamp* (a short progression that repeats over and over), such as Dmin7 to G7, our possibilities narrow to just one modal chord scale: D Dorian. D Dorian is the only mode of the major scale whose chord scale accommodates a minor 7th chord on i and a dominant 7th built on IV. To see this easily, take the major chord scale above and re-order it so that Dmin7 is i. This is the D Dorian chord scale.

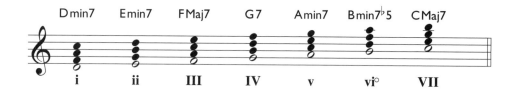

We can use this easy method to create many wonderful little chord vamps for practicing modal improvisation. If you have a sequencer, or any means of home recording, set up the following vamps over which to practice soloing.

If you don't have the means to do this, then just try playing the chords with your left hand while soloing with your right hand. Better yet, find someone to jam with.

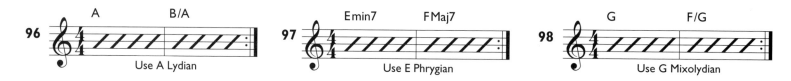

Arpeggios

You can use your knowledge of the chord scales to make arpeggios a tool for improvisation. For example, for our D Dorian vamp (Dmin7 to G7), we have the harmonized chords of the D Dorian chord scale available to arpeggiate. Look at the D Dorian chord scale shown to the right and try arpeggiating each harmony a few different ways. Now, try playing any and all of these arpeggios over the Dorian vamp. Have fun!

Pentatonic Scales

By now, you are well acquainted with both the major and minor pentatonic scales. You know they are five-note scales, derived from the major scale, with these formulas:

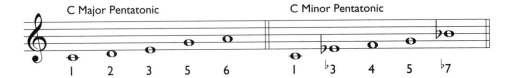

You also know that they relate to each other in much the same way that the major scales relate to their relative minor—C Major pentatonic and A Minor pentatonic have the same notes but in a different order, one starting on C and the other on A.

The major pentatonic scale can be used over any major triad or major 7th chord. The minor pentatonic scale is used over any minor triad or minor 7th chord. Of course, there is always someone ready to throw all caution to the wind and use minor pentatonic scales over major triads and 7th chords, especially in a blues context.

Below is a standard minor 12-bar blues in G, using a dominant chord on V. Try several approaches to improvising over this:

1. Use the G Minor Pentatonic scale throughout.

2. Switch to D Major Pentatonic to play over the V chord, D7.

3. Play the minor pentatonic scale built on the root of each chord: G Minor Pentatonic on Gmin7 chords, C Minor Pentatonic on the Cmin7 chord and D Minor and/or D Major Pentatonic on the D7.

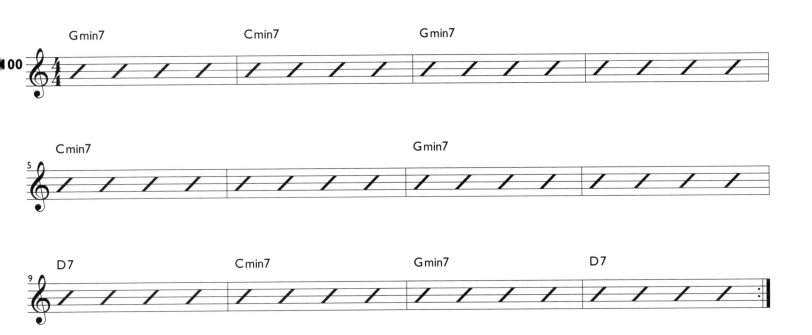

Inflections

Put a personal stamp on your playing. Use dynamics when you play, along with your pitch bend and modulation wheels for bending, sliding and vibrato. These techniques, a good ear, and sense of rhythm separate the great players from the rest.

Diatonic Harmonization of the Melodic and Harmonic Minor Scales

On page 49, we harmonized a C Major scale and talked about its relation to modal harmony (on page 56). Now let's delve into more advanced theory and look at the melodic and harmonic minor scales.

> **Note:** In classical theory, we think of the melodic minor as descending differently than it ascends. It ascends as shown here, and descends in the natural minor. In rock and jazz, we think of it only in the ascending form. This is sometimes called *jazz minor*, but is just as often called *melodic minor*, even though it does not descend in the traditional way.

Melodic Minor

First, let's harmonize the melodic minor scale. Below is a C Melodic Minor chord scale.

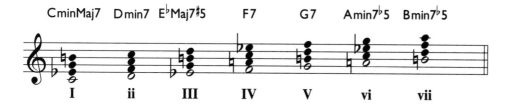

Now, let's take a look at the modes that occur on each degree of the melodic minor scale. These modes are slight variations of the major scale modes. For example, the 2nd mode of the melodic minor scale is just like the Dorian mode of the major scale, except that when compared to the Dorian mode, it has a $^\flat2$. That is why we call it the *Dorian* $^\flat2$.

Modes of the Melodic Minor Scale

Melodic or Jazz Minor Scale

Dorian $^\flat$2 Mode

Lydian $^\sharp$5 Mode

Lydian $^\flat$7 Mode

Mixolydian $^\flat$6 Mode

Aeolian $^\flat$5 Mode

Super Locrian Mode

Harmonic Minor

Now let's take a look at the harmonic minor chord scale (which we first looked at on page 106). Below is a C Harmonic Minor chord scale.

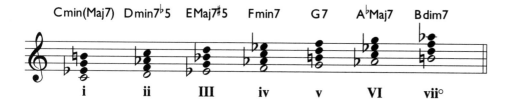

Now let's look at the modes derived from the harmonic minor scale. To the right are the modes of the C Harmonic Minor scale.

Practical application of this information only becomes fluid with a lot of practice. The best way to learn where, when and how to use the correct scales is to analyze other peoples' solos. You should also play along with recorded solos and compose your own (on paper). Also, you must learn to recognize each individual mode when you hear it. Playing modes as scale warm-up exercises will help you do this. Your goal is to become spontaneously inventive with this material.

For your reference, below is a chart showing various chord types and the scales or modes that are appropriate to use when improvising over them.

Modes of the Harmonic Minor Scale

Harmonic Minor Scale

Locrian ♮2 Mode

Ionian ♯5 Mode

Lydian ♭3, ♭7 Mode

Phyrgian Dominant Mode

Lydian ♯2 Mode

7th Mode Harmonic Minor

Chord and Scale Use

Chord Type	Mode or Scale	Chord Type	Mode or Scale
Maj7	Ionian Lydian Lydian ♯2 Major Pentatonic	Unaltered Dominant 7	Mixolydian Lydian ♭7 Mixolydian ♯6 Phrygian Dominant

Chord Type	Mode or Scale	Chord Type	Mode or Scale
Min7	Dorian Phrygian Dorian ♭2 Lydian ♭3 ♭7 Minor Pentatonic	Min7(♭5)	Locrian Aeolian ♭5 Locrian ♯6 Super Locrian* *(usually used in an altered dominant situation)

Chord Type	Mode or Scale	Chord Type	Mode or Scale
Min(Maj7)	Melodic Minor Harmonic Minor	Maj7(♯5)	Lydian ♯5 Ionian ♯5

Chord Type	Mode or Scale
Dim7	7th Mode Harmonic Minor

Modal Interchange and Parallel Modes

Another way to add interest to your music is by introducing non-diatonic notes or chords. In the key of C, for example, you may want to use an A♭ chord. This can be done through *modal interchange*. Modal interchange involves "borrowing" chords from different modes of the same scale-type. We usually don't borrow chords from modes made from other types of scales. If we are in a major key, for instance, we don't usually borrow chords from the modes of the harmonic minor scale. Here's an example: the Aeolian mode is a mode of the major scale. When playing in C Major, if we sneak in a chord from C Aeolian—using another mode of the major scale but keeping the C root—we are applying the principal of *modal interchange*. The chord from C Aeolian, such as A♭, is a *borrowed chord*. We can use C Dorian, C Phrygian, C Lydian, etc. in the same manner. The borrowed chord suggests the sound of its own mode without actually switching to that mode. In theory, any chord from any mode of the scale of the piece is a potential modal interchange or borrowed chord. Some are used more frequently than others, while some almost never occur.

Two of the most common progressions found in rock 'n' roll include modal interchange chords.

The I–♭VII–♭VI–♭VII Progression

The I–♭VII–♭VI–♭VII progression is very common in rock music.

First we have the major I chord, which is diatonic to any major mode. Second is the ♭VII major chord, which gives us a sense that this is a Mixolydian progression, because the Mixolydian mode has the ♭7 degree and the chord built on it is major. Grab a piece of music paper and write out a Mixolydian chord scale—it's a good exercise and you will demonstrate this point for yourself.

But then... the ♭VI major chord. Oh no! This chord does not exist in the Mixolydian mode or any other major mode for that matter! What could it be? It must be a modal interchange chord. There are two modes of the major scale that have a ♭VI major chord: the Aeolian and Phrygian modes. Prove it. Write out the chord scales for those modes.

Play the chords below and hear how this sounds. It will probably sound quite natural since, whether you realize it or not, you've heard this many, many times in rock music.

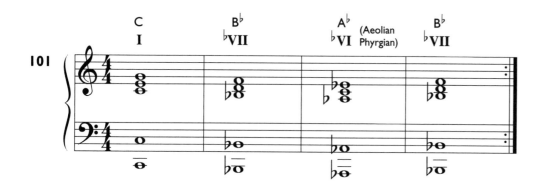

The I–♭VI–IV Progression

Below is a typical major progression with a borrowed ♭VI major chord. Once again, we are borrowing from the Aeolian or Phrygian mode. This progression was used a lot by Yes, Genesis and even Nirvana.

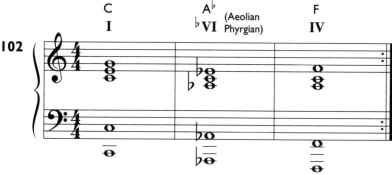

Modal Interchange Cadences

Let's look at some *cadences* that utilize modal interchange. A cadence is the resolution of a progression. It encompasses the chords that end the progression. The example below is a very basic, diatonic chord progression: I major, IV major, V major and back to I major. The last two chords are the cadence because the V major chord resolves back to I major. V major to I major is a commonly used cadence.

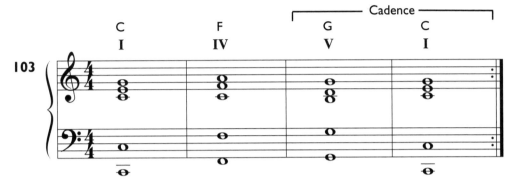

Now, let's substitute a modal interchange, or borrowed chord, for the V chord. We'll hear the same progression as before but with a different cadence. In the example below, the ♭VII major chord from Mixolydian is substituted for the V major chord. This makes a ♭VII major to I major cadence, which is also a very common cadence.

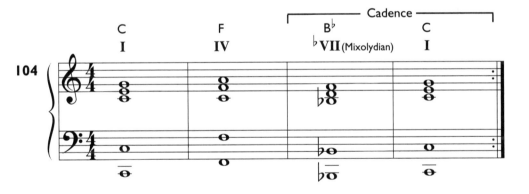

Here are a few more cadences that utilize modal interchange chords:

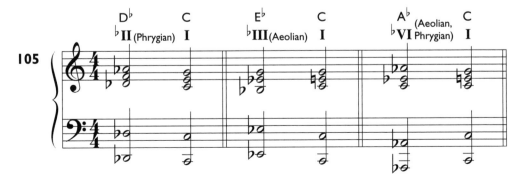

Here's a tune for you to play. This is in the key of D Minor, so it is essentially a D Aeolian (natural minor) progression. The concept of modal interchange works with a minor key, too. Thinking of it as being in D Aeolian leaves you with all of your good old familiar modes of the major scale for use in modal interchange.

Try to find the modal interchange chords. If you found the E♭ Major chord in bars 3 and 7, and the D Major chord in bars 8 and 9, then you are correct. The E♭ Major chord (♭II major) is being borrowed from the parallel Phrygian mode (D Phrygian), and the D Major chord is being borrowed from the parallel Ionian mode (D Major).

Track 73 *Someday*

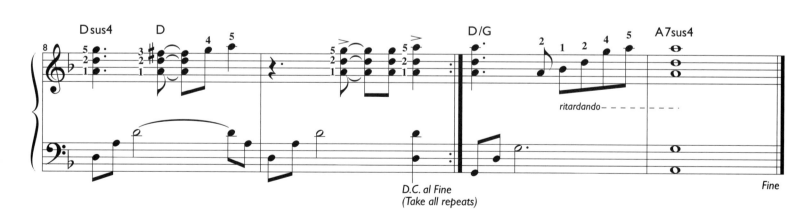

Now, try your hand at a solo. "Moon Beams" is a progressive rock keyboard solo, which sounds great played with a Minimoog sound. The scales or modes being used are indicated in parentheses. This is a D Aeolian progression, but there are also some modal interchange chords. The E7 chord in bars 25 through 28 is borrowed from the parallel Lydian mode (D Lydian) so the note choices are from the A Major scale, the relative major scale to D Lydian. Also, the F#7,11 chord in bars 13 through 20 is functioning as

the V of the B Minor chord, to which it resolves. This is called a *secondary dominant* (any dominant chord that resolves up a 4th but is not part of the key) and it adds a little tension and dissonance to the progression. The chord progression on the CD repeats without the written solo, so you can try playing a solo of your own.

---

tr ⌣ = *Trill.* Rapidly alternate between the note written and the next diatonic note above it. The small notes in parentheses clarify which pitches to use.

Track 74 *Moon Beams*

Chapter 22: Progressive Rock

Progressive rock evolved in the late 1960s and early '70s. It was an era where musical virtuosos brought elements of their classical and jazz backgrounds together with rock instrumentation, early analog synthesizers and odd meters. This style of music is exceptionally exciting to the rock keyboardist because of the challenging parts and featured role the keyboard has in the ensemble.

Odd Meter

Odd meter encompasses time signatures that are not typically used or heard. Since most commercial music is written in standard meters, such as $\frac{4}{4}$, $\frac{3}{4}$, $\frac{6}{8}$, etc., the atypical number of beats per measure found in odd meter time signatures throws a rhythmic curve ball at the listener. Counting an odd meter can be tricky. The most commonly used method is *subdivision*, which means breaking down each measure into smaller rhythmic groups according to how the measure is to be accented. There can be more than one way to subdivide some odd meters.

$\frac{5}{8}$ Time

In $\frac{5}{8}$ time, there are five beats per measure, with the eighth note getting one beat. The following example shows how $\frac{5}{8}$ can be subdivided in two different ways. In the first two bars, beats 1 and 3 are accented. This splits the measure into one group of two eighth notes and one group of three eighth notes. Instead of counting to "5" for each measure, each subdivision is counted separately (1-2, 1-2-3). The second two bars are subdivided in the opposite way, counted (1–2–3, 1–2). The subdivisions are shown using *rhythmic notation*. Slashes are used instead of regular noteheads to indicate rhythm without specifying pitch.

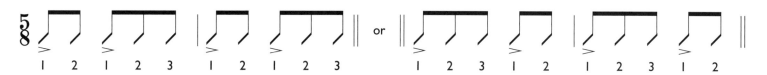

$\frac{7}{8}$ Time

In $\frac{7}{8}$ there are seven beats per measure and the eighth note gets one beat. The following examples show four different ways to subdivide this meter.

$\frac{5}{4}$ Time

In $\frac{5}{4}$ there are five beats per measure and a quarter note gets one beat. You can still subdivide with eighth notes if you like. The example below uses a subdivision other than quarter notes. Below, you see beats 1, 2, 3 and the "&" of 4 accented (with eighth notes, you can count it like this: 1-2, 1-2, 1-2-3, 1-2-3).

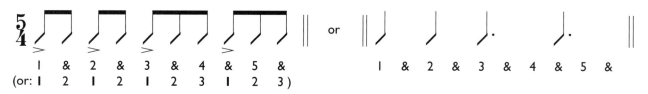

The band Rush doesn't have a full-time keyboard player (in concert, the band members trigger synth parts with foot pedals), yet they've been a huge influence in the progressive rock movement. Their keyboard parts tend to be more thematic than solo-oriented.

"Sub-Plots" is in the style of Rush's "Subdivisions," which has what is probably the closest they ever came to a keyboard solo. Try using a synth with a solid string sound and a quick attack time.

Like many progressive rock songs, this one changes time signatures frequently. The trick here is to keep the quarter-note pulse steady, whether there are seven beats per measure ($\frac{7}{4}$), five beats per measure ($\frac{5}{4}$), four beats per measure ($\frac{4}{4}$) or six beats per measure ($\frac{6}{4}$). Once you feel this beat, count the correct number of beats for each measure, and you'll be able to keep up with the shifting time signatures.

Track 76 *Sub-Plots*

Let's take a look at the style of Yes keyboard virtuoso, Rick Wakeman. He is a classically trained pianist who developed a taste (not to mention talent) for blues and jazz. Legend has it that, as a student at the Royal Academy of Music in London, he used to sneak out, against school policy, to make extra money playing on studio sessions.

The following example is in the style of one of the Moog solos from "The Revealing Signs of God," which is 29 minutes long. The extensive use of trills exemplifies Wakeman's classical influence.

The trills in this song are notated as follows:

Track 77 *Forces of Heaven*

"Wake Up" also demonstrates Wakeman's classical influences. It is in the style of the piano part in "Catherine of Aragon" from his solo album *The Six Wives of Henry VIII*.

Track 78 *Wake Up*

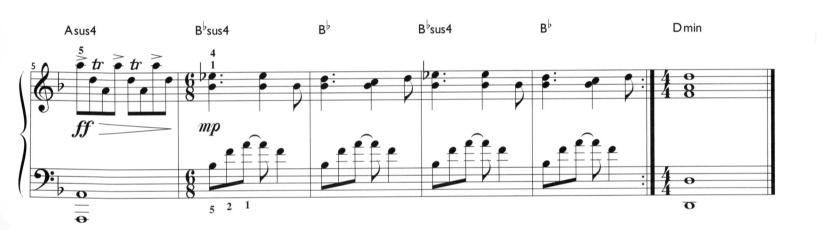

Conclusion

While this is the end of the book, it isn't the end of the story. Playing rock keyboard is a lifelong pursuit that will give you a sense of accomplishment and lots of enjoyment. This book got you started with the basic tools. By now, you are a rockin' keyboard player. There's a lot left to learn, though, so never stop listening, learning and practicing. Branch out to other styles of music such as classical and jazz, and always be open to new influences. Keep the music going, and have fun!